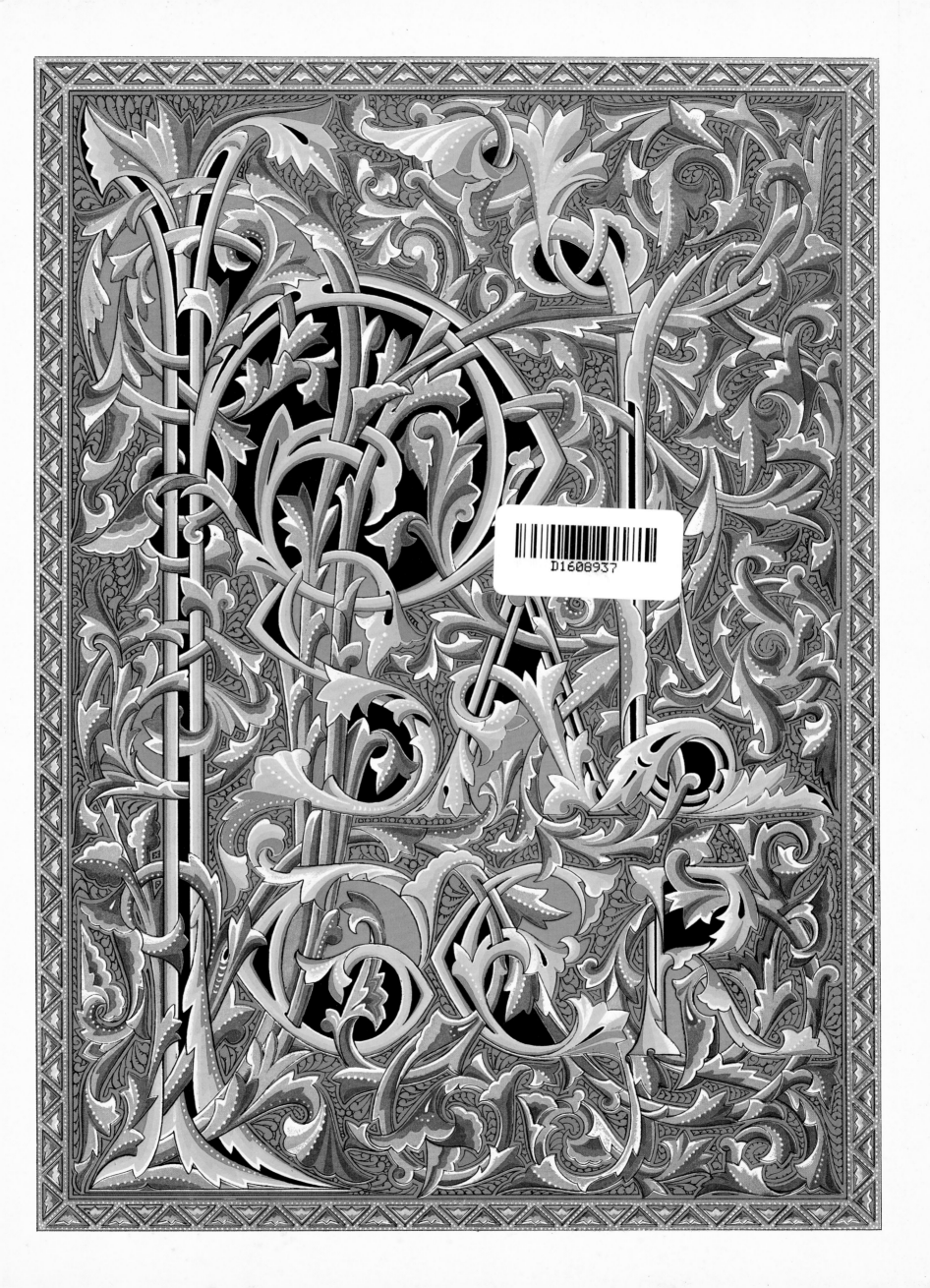

THE PSALMS

---◆---

OF DAVID

THE PSALMS

◆

OF DAVID

The great illuminated psalter dedicated to Queen Victoria
— *by* —

OWEN JONES

GALLERY BOOKS
An Imprint of W. H. Smith Publishers Inc.
112 Madison Avenue
New York, New York 10016

This edition published 1989 by Gallery Books,
an imprint of W.H. Smith Publishers Inc,
112 Madison Avenue, New York, New York 10016.

Copyright © Wordsworth Editions 1989.

All rights reserved.

ISBN 1-8317-7130-5

Printed and bound in Spain by Gráficas Estella SA.

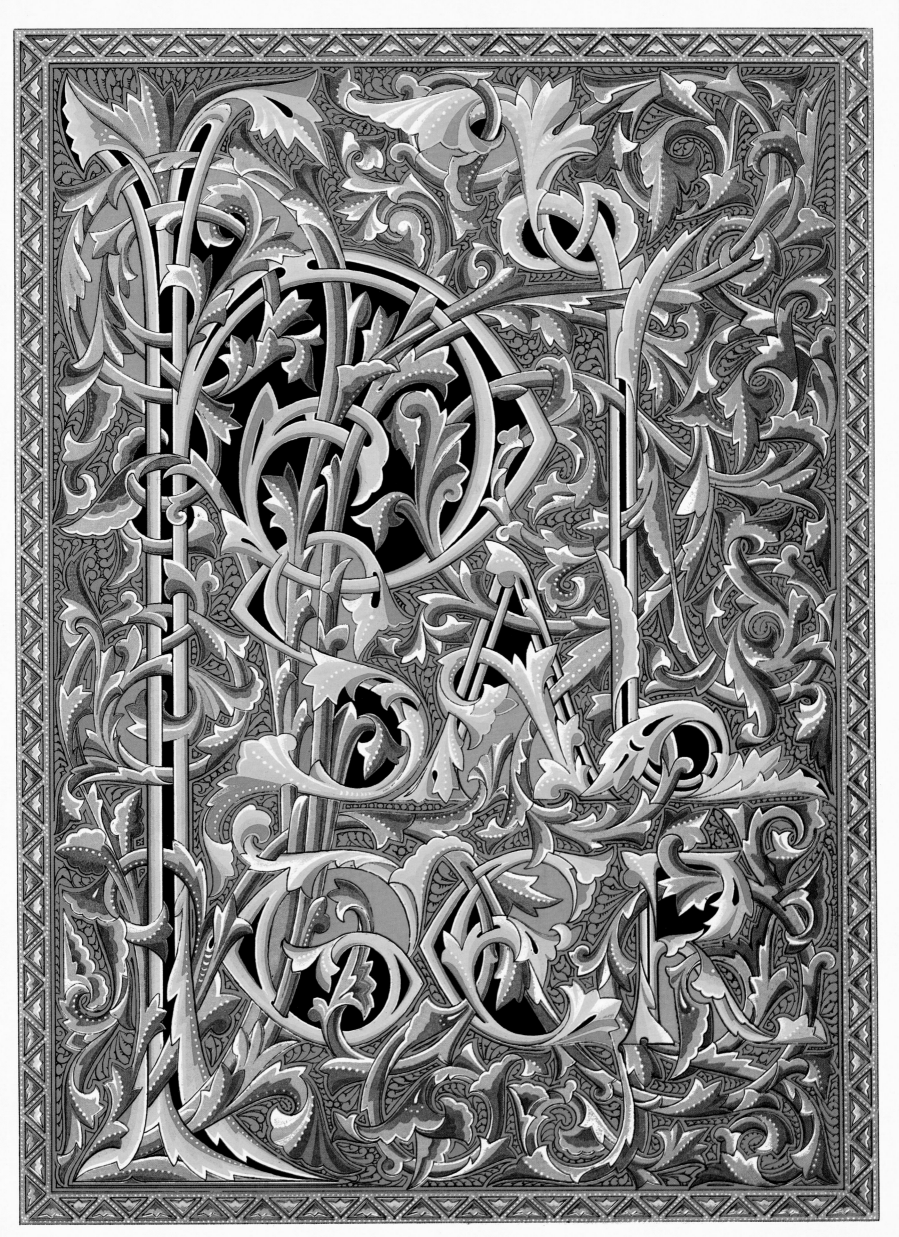

V.

THE

PSALMS OF DAVID

Illuminated

by

OWEN JONES

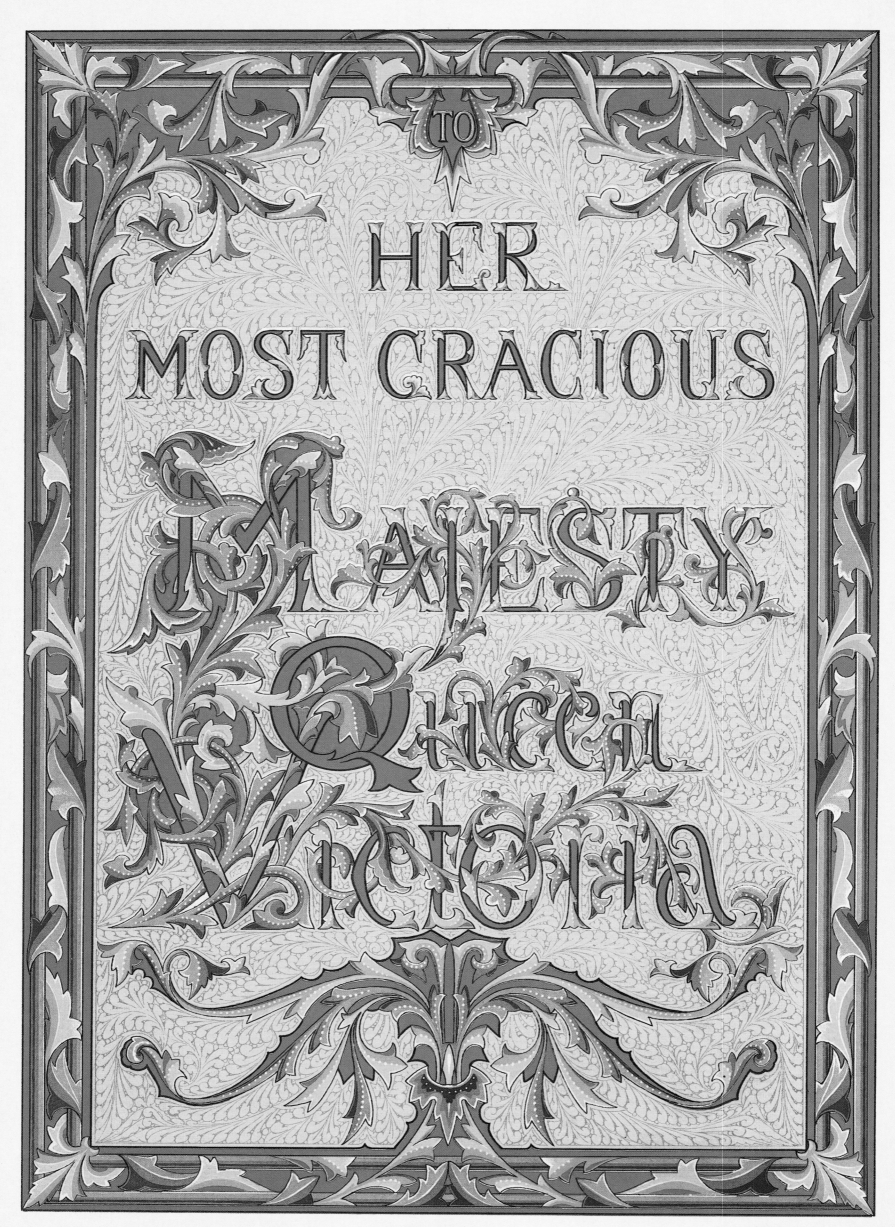

TO
HER
MOST GRACIOUS
MAJESTY
QUEEN
VICTORIA

VIII.

THIS
ILLUMINATED
PSALTER
✝
with permission
Dedicated

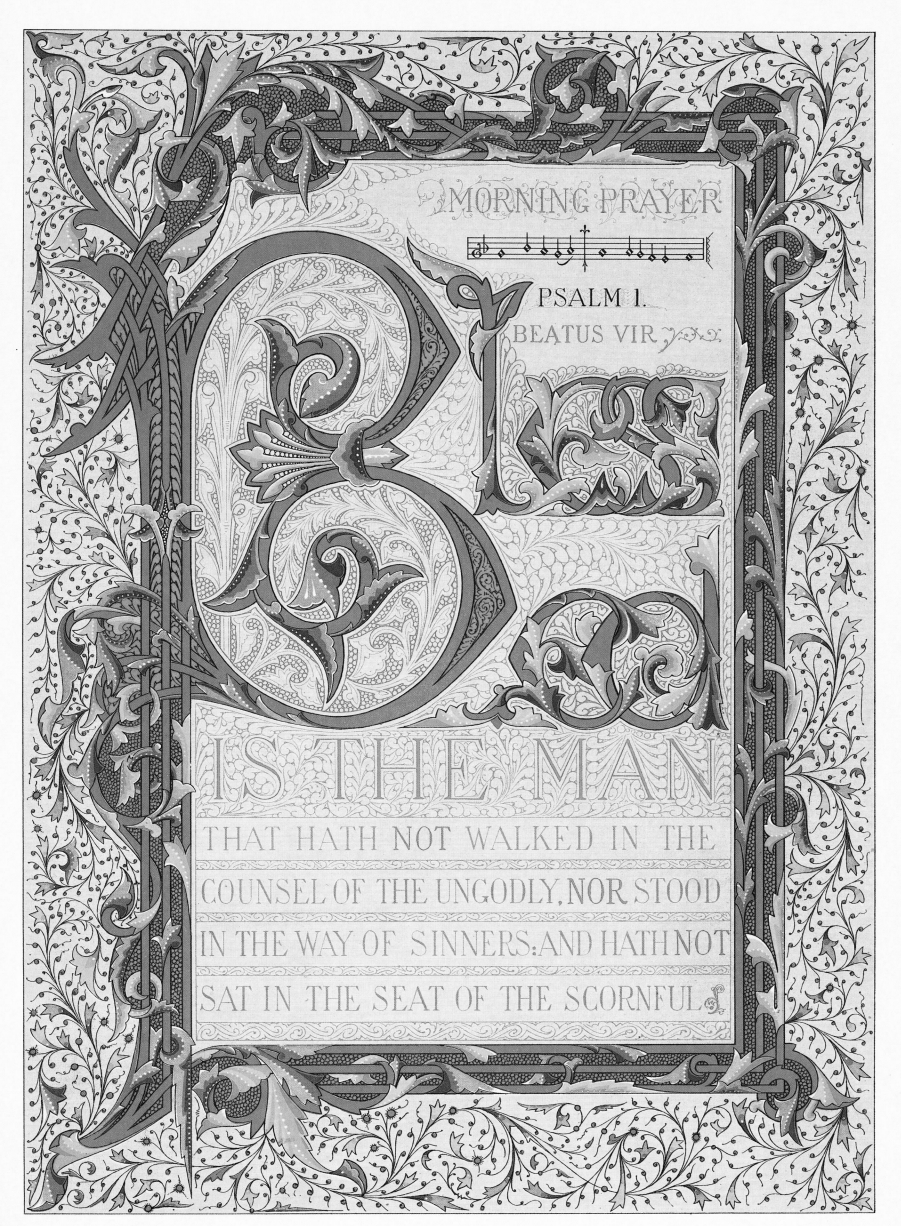

MORNING PRAYER

PSALM I.

BEATUS VIR.

Blessed IS THE MAN THAT HATH NOT WALKED IN THE COUNSEL OF THE UNGODLY, NOR STOOD IN THE WAY OF SINNERS: AND HATH NOT SAT IN THE SEAT OF THE SCORNFUL.

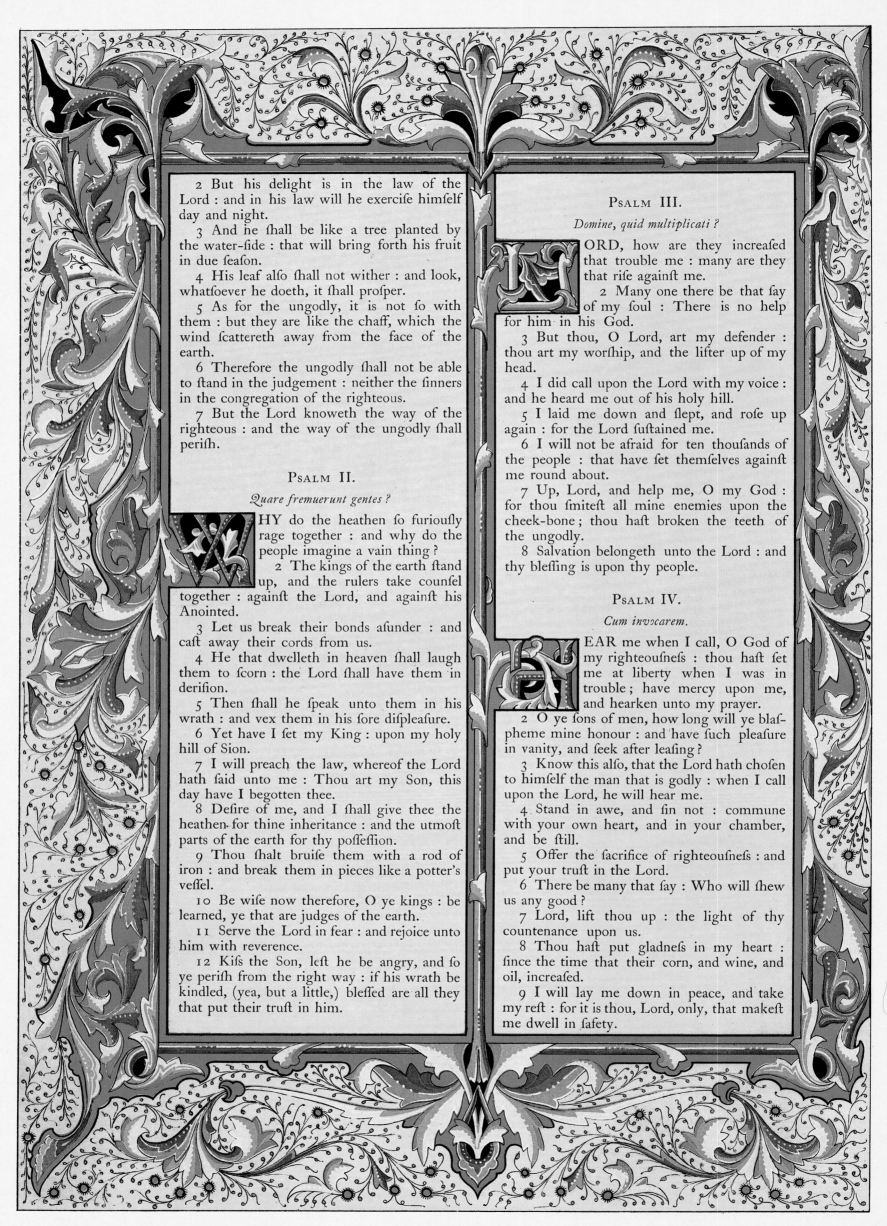

2 But his delight is in the law of the Lord : and in his law will he exercise himself day and night.

3 And he shall be like a tree planted by the water-side : that will bring forth his fruit in due season.

4 His leaf also shall not wither : and look, whatsoever he doeth, it shall prosper.

5 As for the ungodly, it is not so with them : but they are like the chaff, which the wind scattereth away from the face of the earth.

6 Therefore the ungodly shall not be able to stand in the judgement : neither the sinners in the congregation of the righteous.

7 But the Lord knoweth the way of the righteous : and the way of the ungodly shall perish.

Psalm II.

Quare fremuerunt gentes?

WHY do the heathen so furiously rage together : and why do the people imagine a vain thing?

2 The kings of the earth stand up, and the rulers take counsel together : against the Lord, and against his Anointed.

3 Let us break their bonds asunder : and cast away their cords from us.

4 He that dwelleth in heaven shall laugh them to scorn : the Lord shall have them in derision.

5 Then shall he speak unto them in his wrath : and vex them in his sore displeasure.

6 Yet have I set my King : upon my holy hill of Sion.

7 I will preach the law, whereof the Lord hath said unto me : Thou art my Son, this day have I begotten thee.

8 Desire of me, and I shall give thee the heathen for thine inheritance : and the utmost parts of the earth for thy possession.

9 Thou shalt bruise them with a rod of iron : and break them in pieces like a potter's vessel.

10 Be wise now therefore, O ye kings : be learned, ye that are judges of the earth.

11 Serve the Lord in fear : and rejoice unto him with reverence.

12 Kiss the Son, lest he be angry, and so ye perish from the right way : if his wrath be kindled, (yea, but a little,) blessed are all they that put their trust in him.

Psalm III.

Domine, quid multiplicati?

LORD, how are they increased that trouble me : many are they that rise against me.

2 Many one there be that say of my soul : There is no help for him in his God.

3 But thou, O Lord, art my defender : thou art my worship, and the lifter up of my head.

4 I did call upon the Lord with my voice : and he heard me out of his holy hill.

5 I laid me down and slept, and rose up again : for the Lord sustained me.

6 I will not be afraid for ten thousands of the people : that have set themselves against me round about.

7 Up, Lord, and help me, O my God : for thou smitest all mine enemies upon the cheek-bone ; thou hast broken the teeth of the ungodly.

8 Salvation belongeth unto the Lord : and thy blessing is upon thy people.

Psalm IV.

Cum invocarem.

HEAR me when I call, O God of my righteousness : thou hast set me at liberty when I was in trouble ; have mercy upon me, and hearken unto my prayer.

2 O ye sons of men, how long will ye blaspheme mine honour : and have such pleasure in vanity, and seek after leasing?

3 Know this also, that the Lord hath chosen to himself the man that is godly : when I call upon the Lord, he will hear me.

4 Stand in awe, and sin not : commune with your own heart, and in your chamber, and be still.

5 Offer the sacrifice of righteousness : and put your trust in the Lord.

6 There be many that say : Who will shew us any good?

7 Lord, lift thou up : the light of thy countenance upon us.

8 Thou hast put gladness in my heart : since the time that their corn, and wine, and oil, increased.

9 I will lay me down in peace, and take my rest : for it is thou, Lord, only, that makest me dwell in safety.

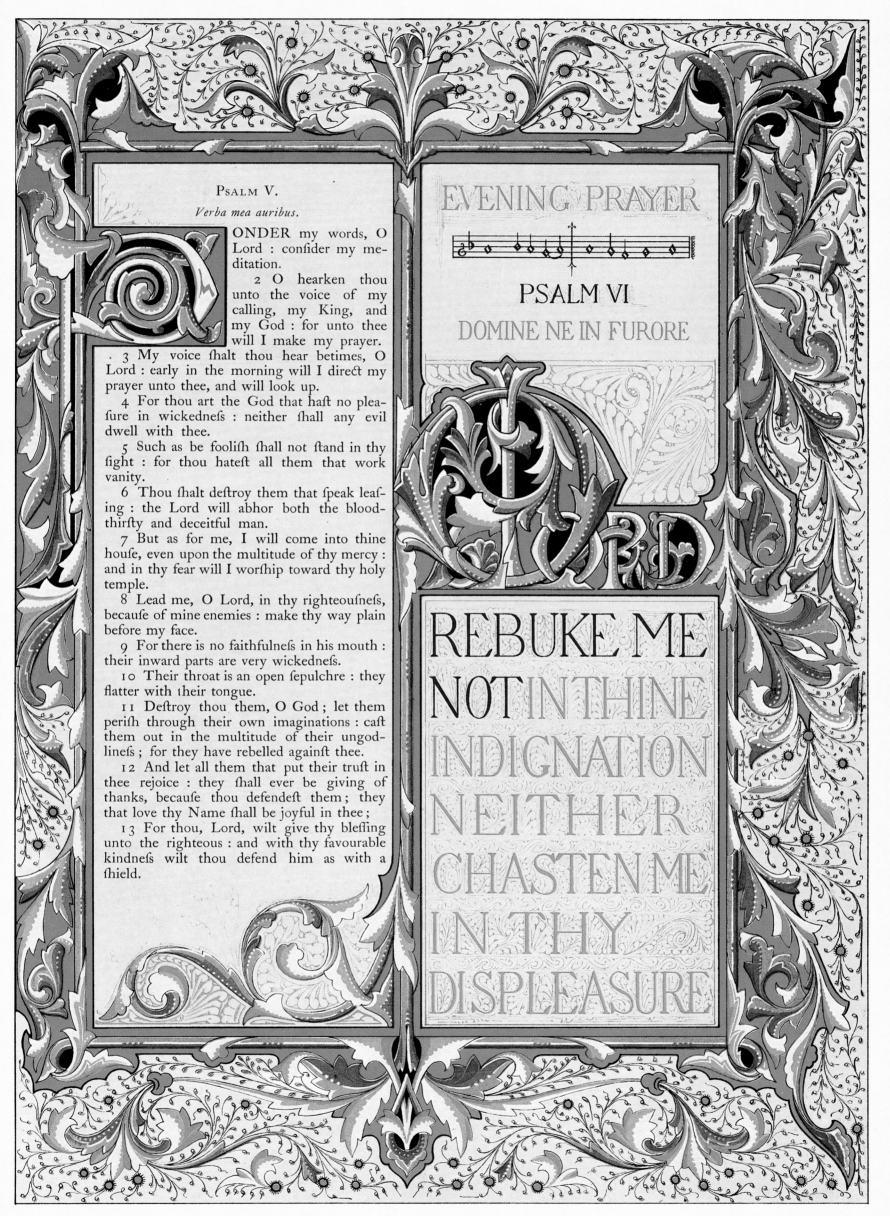

PSALM V.
Verba mea auribus.

PONDER my words, O Lord : confider my meditation.

2 O hearken thou unto the voice of my calling, my King, and my God : for unto thee will I make my prayer.

3 My voice fhalt thou hear betimes, O Lord : early in the morning will I direct my prayer unto thee, and will look up.

4 For thou art the God that haft no pleafure in wickednefs : neither fhall any evil dwell with thee.

5 Such as be foolifh fhall not ftand in thy fight : for thou hateft all them that work vanity.

6 Thou fhalt deftroy them that fpeak leafing : the Lord will abhor both the bloodthirfty and deceitful man.

7 But as for me, I will come into thine houfe, even upon the multitude of thy mercy : and in thy fear will I worfhip toward thy holy temple.

8 Lead me, O Lord, in thy righteoufnefs, becaufe of mine enemies : make thy way plain before my face.

9 For there is no faithfulnefs in his mouth : their inward parts are very wickednefs.

10 Their throat is an open fepulchre : they flatter with their tongue.

11 Deftroy thou them, O God ; let them perifh through their own imaginations : caft them out in the multitude of their ungodlinefs ; for they have rebelled againft thee.

12 And let all them that put their truft in thee rejoice : they fhall ever be giving of thanks, becaufe thou defendeft them ; they that love thy Name fhall be joyful in thee ;

13 For thou, Lord, wilt give thy bleffing unto the righteous : and with thy favourable kindnefs wilt thou defend him as with a fhield.

EVENING PRAYER

PSALM VI

DOMINE NE IN FURORE

O LORD REBUKE ME NOT IN THINE INDIGNATION NEITHER CHASTEN ME IN THY DISPLEASURE

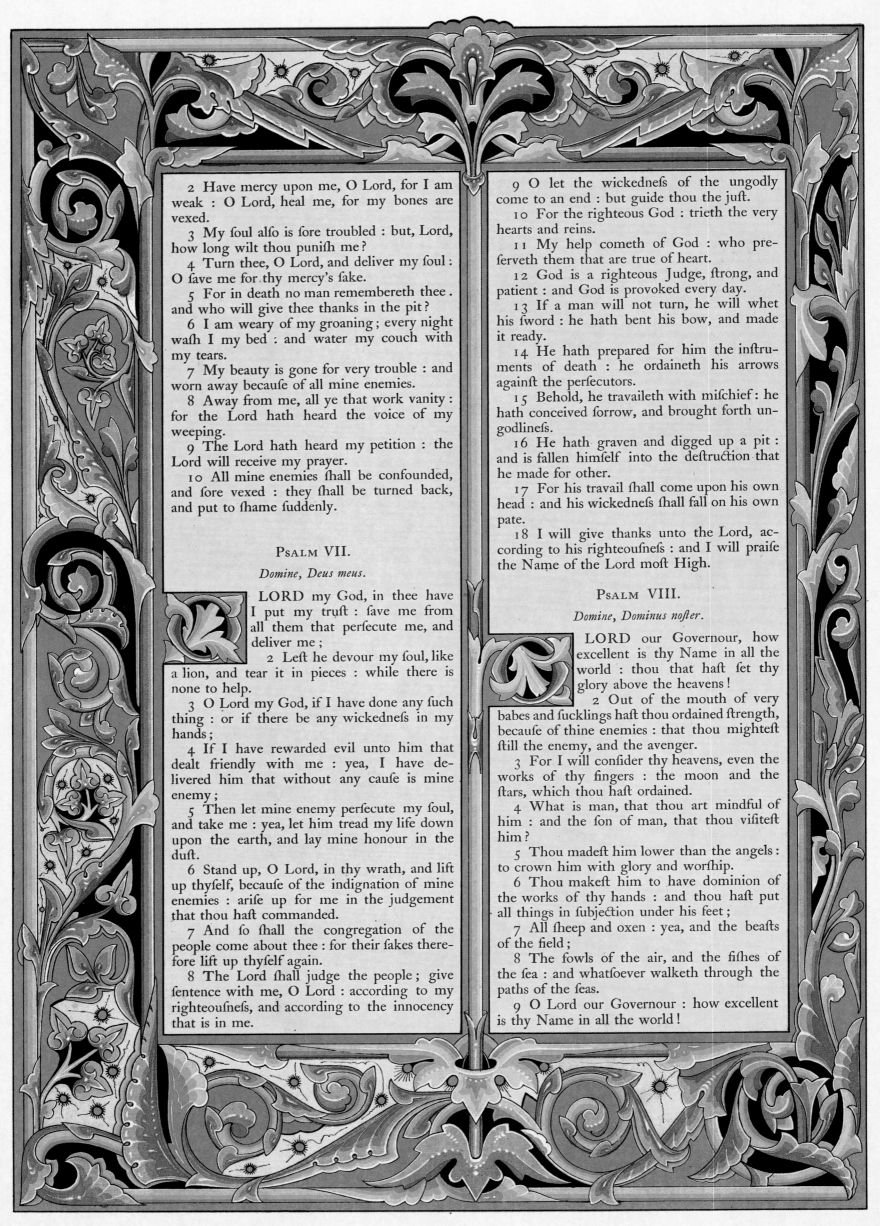

2 Have mercy upon me, O Lord, for I am weak : O Lord, heal me, for my bones are vexed.

3 My soul also is sore troubled : but, Lord, how long wilt thou punish me?

4 Turn thee, O Lord, and deliver my soul : O save me for thy mercy's sake.

5 For in death no man remembereth thee . and who will give thee thanks in the pit?

6 I am weary of my groaning; every night wash I my bed : and water my couch with my tears.

7 My beauty is gone for very trouble : and worn away because of all mine enemies.

8 Away from me, all ye that work vanity : for the Lord hath heard the voice of my weeping.

9 The Lord hath heard my petition : the Lord will receive my prayer.

10 All mine enemies shall be confounded, and sore vexed : they shall be turned back, and put to shame suddenly.

Psalm VII.
Domine, Deus meus.

LORD my God, in thee have I put my trust : save me from all them that persecute me, and deliver me ;

2 Lest he devour my soul, like a lion, and tear it in pieces : while there is none to help.

3 O Lord my God, if I have done any such thing : or if there be any wickedness in my hands ;

4 If I have rewarded evil unto him that dealt friendly with me : yea, I have delivered him that without any cause is mine enemy ;

5 Then let mine enemy persecute my soul, and take me : yea, let him tread my life down upon the earth, and lay mine honour in the dust.

6 Stand up, O Lord, in thy wrath, and lift up thyself, because of the indignation of mine enemies : arise up for me in the judgement that thou hast commanded.

7 And so shall the congregation of the people come about thee : for their sakes therefore lift up thyself again.

8 The Lord shall judge the people ; give sentence with me, O Lord : according to my righteousness, and according to the innocency that is in me.

9 O let the wickedness of the ungodly come to an end : but guide thou the just.

10 For the righteous God : trieth the very hearts and reins.

11 My help cometh of God : who preserveth them that are true of heart.

12 God is a righteous Judge, strong, and patient : and God is provoked every day.

13 If a man will not turn, he will whet his sword : he hath bent his bow, and made it ready.

14 He hath prepared for him the instruments of death : he ordaineth his arrows against the persecutors.

15 Behold, he travaileth with mischief : he hath conceived sorrow, and brought forth ungodliness.

16 He hath graven and digged up a pit : and is fallen himself into the destruction that he made for other.

17 For his travail shall come upon his own head : and his wickedness shall fall on his own pate.

18 I will give thanks unto the Lord, according to his righteousness : and I will praise the Name of the Lord most High.

Psalm VIII.
Domine, Dominus noster.

LORD our Governour, how excellent is thy Name in all the world : thou that hast set thy glory above the heavens !

2 Out of the mouth of very babes and sucklings hast thou ordained strength, because of thine enemies : that thou mightest still the enemy, and the avenger.

3 For I will consider thy heavens, even the works of thy fingers : the moon and the stars, which thou hast ordained.

4 What is man, that thou art mindful of him : and the son of man, that thou visitest him ?

5 Thou madest him lower than the angels : to crown him with glory and worship.

6 Thou makest him to have dominion of the works of thy hands : and thou hast put all things in subjection under his feet ;

7 All sheep and oxen : yea, and the beasts of the field ;

8 The fowls of the air, and the fishes of the sea : and whatsoever walketh through the paths of the seas.

9 O Lord our Governour : how excellent is thy Name in all the world !

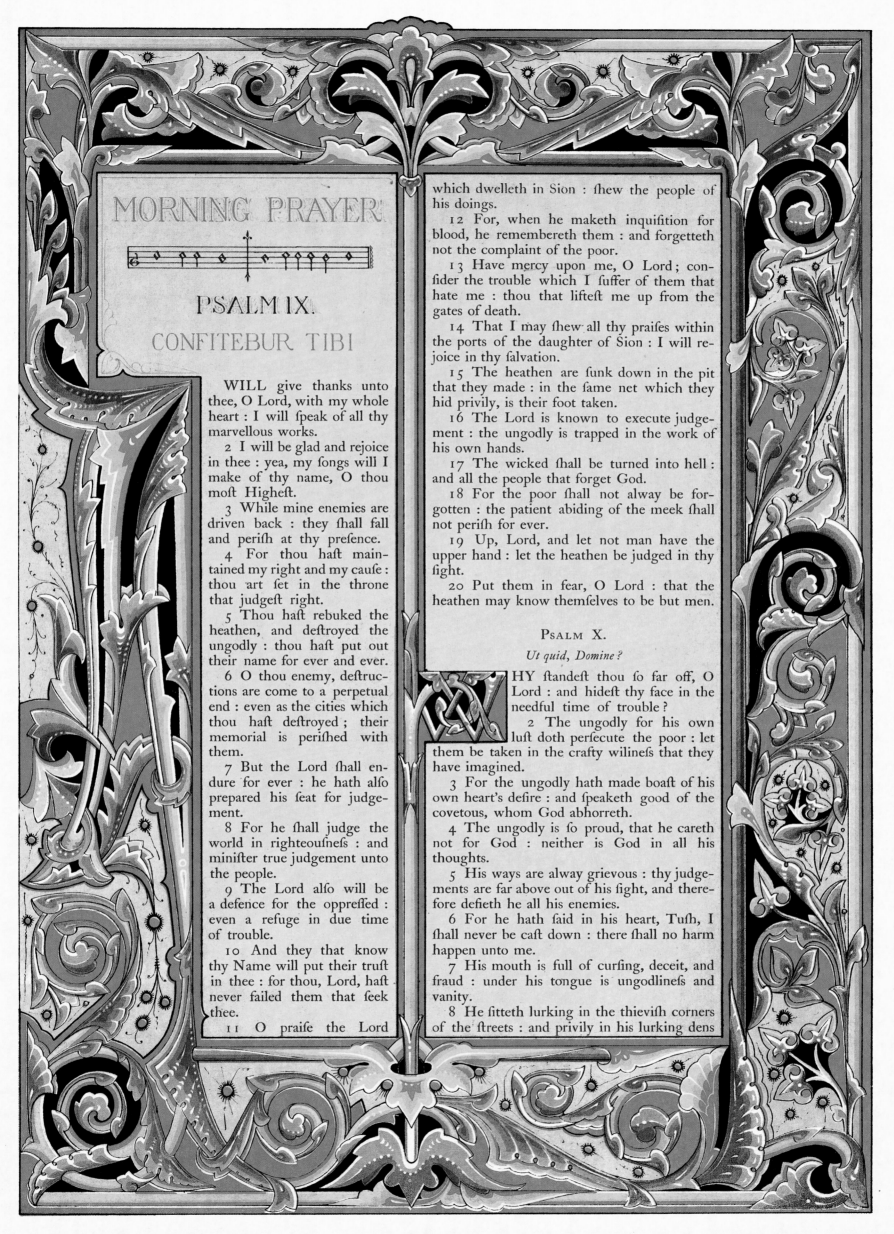

MORNING PRAYER.

PSALM IX.

CONFITEBUR TIBI.

WILL give thanks unto thee, O Lord, with my whole heart : I will speak of all thy marvellous works.

2 I will be glad and rejoice in thee : yea, my songs will I make of thy name, O thou most Higheſt.

3 While mine enemies are driven back : they ſhall fall and periſh at thy preſence.

4 For thou haſt maintained my right and my cauſe : thou art ſet in the throne that judgeſt right.

5 Thou haſt rebuked the heathen, and deſtroyed the ungodly : thou haſt put out their name for ever and ever.

6 O thou enemy, deſtructions are come to a perpetual end : even as the cities which thou haſt deſtroyed ; their memorial is periſhed with them.

7 But the Lord ſhall endure for ever : he hath alſo prepared his ſeat for judgement.

8 For he ſhall judge the world in righteouſneſs : and miniſter true judgement unto the people.

9 The Lord alſo will be a defence for the oppreſſed : even a refuge in due time of trouble.

10 And they that know thy Name will put their truſt in thee : for thou, Lord, haſt never failed them that ſeek thee.

11 O praiſe the Lord which dwelleth in Sion : ſhew the people of his doings.

12 For, when he maketh inquiſition for blood, he remembereth them : and forgetteth not the complaint of the poor.

13 Have mercy upon me, O Lord ; conſider the trouble which I ſuffer of them that hate me : thou that lifteſt me up from the gates of death.

14 That I may ſhew all thy praiſes within the ports of the daughter of Sion : I will rejoice in thy ſalvation.

15 The heathen are ſunk down in the pit that they made : in the ſame net which they hid privily, is their foot taken.

16 The Lord is known to execute judgement : the ungodly is trapped in the work of his own hands.

17 The wicked ſhall be turned into hell : and all the people that forget God.

18 For the poor ſhall not alway be forgotten : the patient abiding of the meek ſhall not periſh for ever.

19 Up, Lord, and let not man have the upper hand : let the heathen be judged in thy ſight.

20 Put them in fear, O Lord : that the heathen may know themſelves to be but men.

PSALM X.

Ut quid, Domine?

HY ſtandeſt thou ſo far off, O Lord : and hideſt thy face in the needful time of trouble?

2 The ungodly for his own luſt doth perſecute the poor : let them be taken in the crafty wilineſs that they have imagined.

3 For the ungodly hath made boaſt of his own heart's deſire : and ſpeaketh good of the covetous, whom God abhorreth.

4 The ungodly is ſo proud, that he careth not for God : neither is God in all his thoughts.

5 His ways are alway grievous : thy judgements are far above out of his ſight, and therefore defieth he all his enemies.

6 For he hath ſaid in his heart, Tuſh, I ſhall never be caſt down : there ſhall no harm happen unto me.

7 His mouth is full of curſing, deceit, and fraud : under his tongue is ungodlineſs and vanity.

8 He ſitteth lurking in the thieviſh corners of the ſtreets : and privily in his lurking dens

doth he murder the innocent; his eyes are set againſt the poor.

9 For he lieth waiting ſecretly, even as a lion lurketh he in his den : that he may raviſh the poor.

10 He doth raviſh the poor : when he getteth him into his net.

11 He falleth down, and humbleth himſelf : that the congregation of the poor may fall into the hands of his captains.

12 He hath ſaid in his heart, Tuſh, God hath forgotten : he hideth away his face, and he will never ſee it.

13 Ariſe, O Lord God, and lift up thine hand : forget not the poor.

14 Wherefore ſhould the wicked blaſpheme God : while he doth ſay in his heart, Tuſh, thou God careſt not for it.

15 Surely thou haſt ſeen it : for thou beholdeſt ungodlineſs and wrong.

16 That thou mayeſt take the matter into thine hand : the poor committeth himſelf unto thee; for thou art the helper of the friendleſs.

17 Break thou the power of the ungodly and malicious : take away his ungodlineſs, and thou ſhalt find none.

18 The Lord is King for ever and ever : and the heathen are periſhed out of the land.

19 Lord, thou haſt heard the deſire of the poor : thou prepareſt their heart, and thine ear hearkeneth thereto ;

20 To help the fatherleſs and poor unto their right : that the man of the earth be no more exalted againſt them.

Psalm XI.

In Domino confido.

N the Lord put I my truſt : how ſay ye then to my ſoul, that ſhe ſhould flee as a bird unto the hill?

2 For lo, the ungodly bend their bow, and make ready their arrows within the quiver : that they may privily ſhoot at them which are true of heart.

3 For the foundations will be caſt down : and what hath the righteous done?

4 The Lord is in his holy temple : the Lord's ſeat is in heaven.

5 His eyes conſider the poor : and his eyelids try the children of men.

6 The Lord alloweth the righteous : but the ungodly, and him that delighteth in wickedneſs doth his ſoul abhor.

7 Upon the ungodly he ſhall rain ſnares, fire and brimſtone, ſtorm and tempeſt : this ſhall be their portion to drink.

8 For the righteous Lord loveth righteouſneſs : his countenance will behold the thing that is juſt.

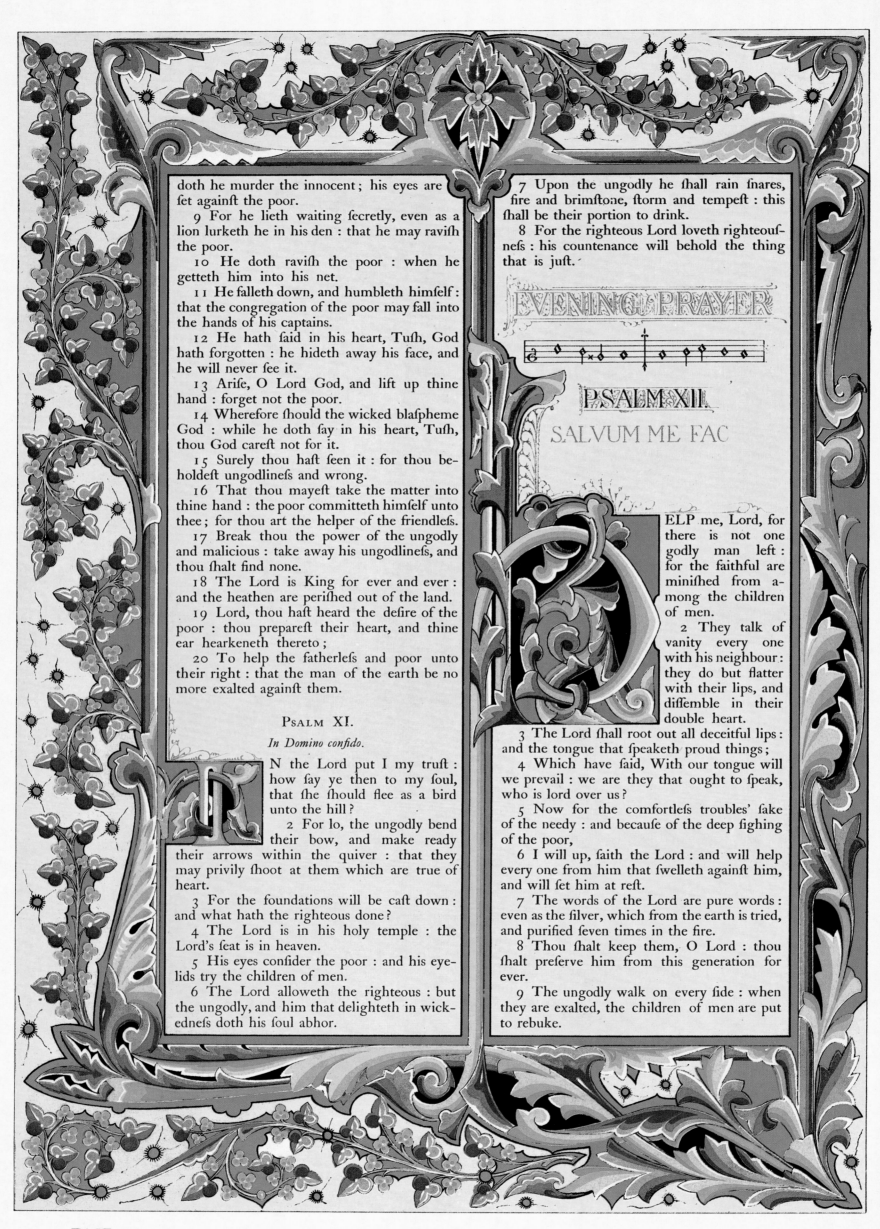

EVENING PRAYER

PSALM XII.

SALVUM ME FAC

ELP me, Lord, for there is not one godly man left : for the faithful are miniſhed from among the children of men.

2 They talk of vanity every one with his neighbour : they do but flatter with their lips, and diſſemble in their double heart.

3 The Lord ſhall root out all deceitful lips : and the tongue that ſpeaketh proud things;

4 Which have ſaid, With our tongue will we prevail : we are they that ought to ſpeak, who is lord over us?

5 Now for the comfortleſs troubles' ſake of the needy : and becauſe of the deep ſighing of the poor,

6 I will up, ſaith the Lord : and will help every one from him that ſwelleth againſt him, and will ſet him at reſt.

7 The words of the Lord are pure words : even as the ſilver, which from the earth is tried, and purified ſeven times in the fire.

8 Thou ſhalt keep them, O Lord : thou ſhalt preſerve him from this generation for ever.

9 The ungodly walk on every ſide : when they are exalted, the children of men are put to rebuke.

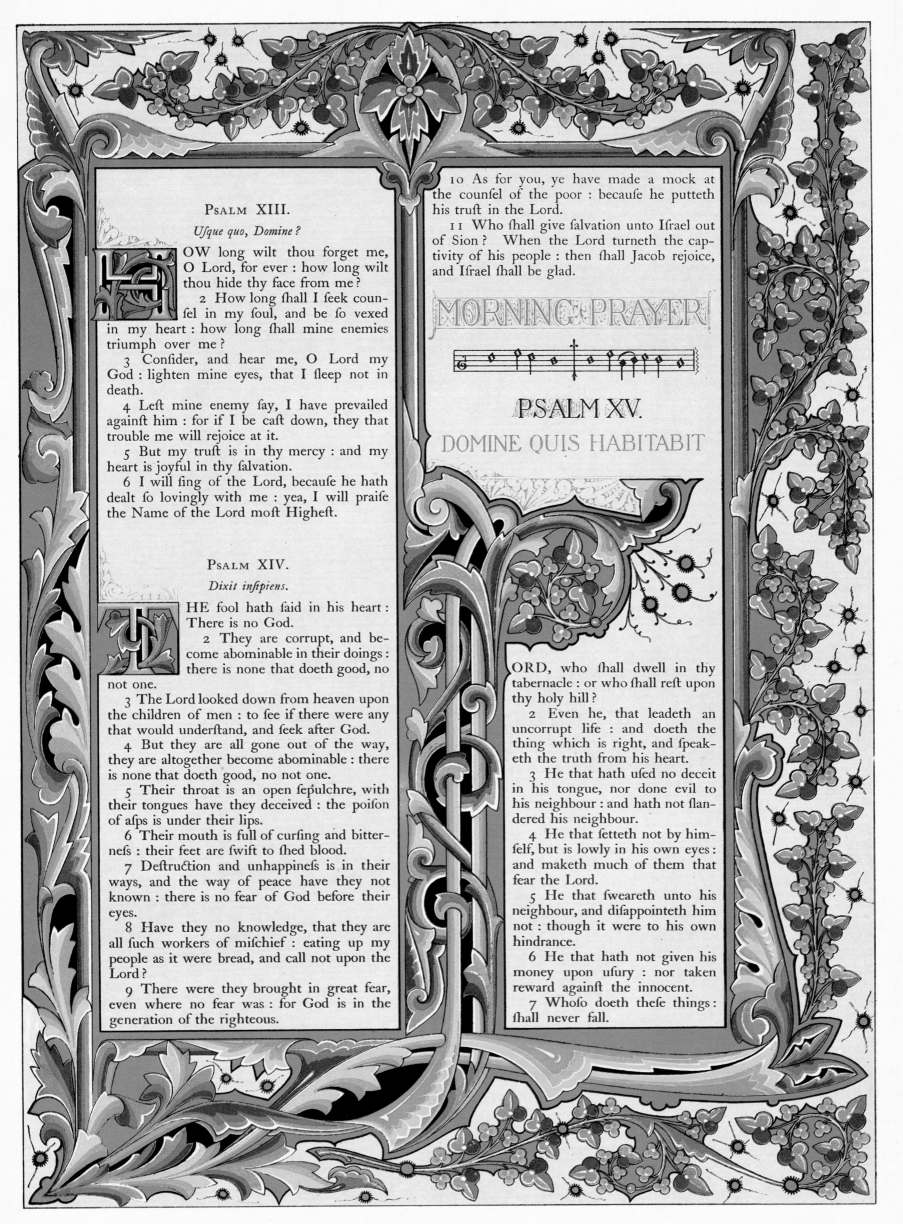

Psalm XIII.

Ufque quo, Domine?

OW long wilt thou forget me, O Lord, for ever : how long wilt thou hide thy face from me?

2 How long shall I seek counsel in my soul, and be so vexed in my heart : how long shall mine enemies triumph over me?

3 Consider, and hear me, O Lord my God : lighten mine eyes, that I sleep not in death.

4 Lest mine enemy say, I have prevailed against him : for if I be cast down, they that trouble me will rejoice at it.

5 But my trust is in thy mercy : and my heart is joyful in thy salvation.

6 I will sing of the Lord, because he hath dealt so lovingly with me : yea, I will praise the Name of the Lord most Highest.

Psalm XIV.

Dixit insipiens.

HE fool hath said in his heart : There is no God.

2 They are corrupt, and become abominable in their doings : there is none that doeth good, no not one.

3 The Lord looked down from heaven upon the children of men : to see if there were any that would understand, and seek after God.

4 But they are all gone out of the way, they are altogether become abominable : there is none that doeth good, no not one.

5 Their throat is an open sepulchre, with their tongues have they deceived : the poison of asps is under their lips.

6 Their mouth is full of cursing and bitterness : their feet are swift to shed blood.

7 Destruction and unhappiness is in their ways, and the way of peace have they not known : there is no fear of God before their eyes.

8 Have they no knowledge, that they are all such workers of mischief : eating up my people as it were bread, and call not upon the Lord?

9 There were they brought in great fear, even where no fear was : for God is in the generation of the righteous.

10 As for you, ye have made a mock at the counsel of the poor : because he putteth his trust in the Lord.

11 Who shall give salvation unto Israel out of Sion? When the Lord turneth the captivity of his people : then shall Jacob rejoice, and Israel shall be glad.

MORNING PRAYER

PSALM XV.

DOMINE QUIS HABITABIT

ORD, who shall dwell in thy tabernacle : or who shall rest upon thy holy hill?

2 Even he, that leadeth an uncorrupt life : and doeth the thing which is right, and speaketh the truth from his heart.

3 He that hath used no deceit in his tongue, nor done evil to his neighbour : and hath not slandered his neighbour.

4 He that setteth not by himself, but is lowly in his own eyes : and maketh much of them that fear the Lord.

5 He that sweareth unto his neighbour, and disappointeth him not : though it were to his own hindrance.

6 He that hath not given his money upon usury : nor taken reward against the innocent.

7 Whoso doeth these things : shall never fall.

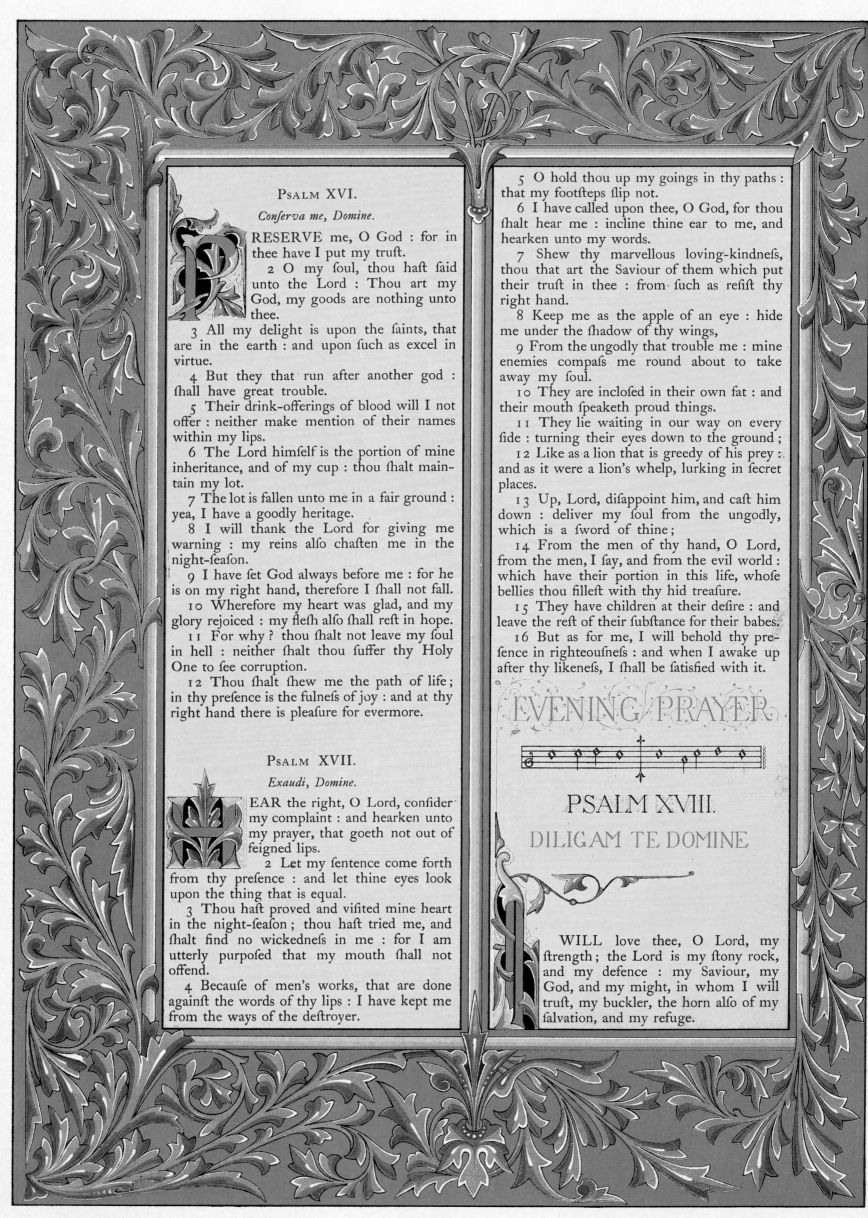

Psalm XVI.

Conserva me, Domine.

PRESERVE me, O God : for in thee have I put my truft.

2 O my foul, thou haft faid unto the Lord : Thou art my God, my goods are nothing unto thee.

3 All my delight is upon the faints, that are in the earth : and upon fuch as excel in virtue.

4 But they that run after another god : fhall have great trouble.

5 Their drink-offerings of blood will I not offer : neither make mention of their names within my lips.

6 The Lord himfelf is the portion of mine inheritance, and of my cup : thou fhalt maintain my lot.

7 The lot is fallen unto me in a fair ground : yea, I have a goodly heritage.

8 I will thank the Lord for giving me warning : my reins alfo chaften me in the night-feafon.

9 I have fet God always before me : for he is on my right hand, therefore I fhall not fall.

10 Wherefore my heart was glad, and my glory rejoiced : my flefh alfo fhall reft in hope.

11 For why ? thou fhalt not leave my foul in hell : neither fhalt thou fuffer thy Holy One to fee corruption.

12 Thou fhalt fhew me the path of life ; in thy prefence is the fulnefs of joy : and at thy right hand there is pleafure for evermore.

Psalm XVII.

Exaudi, Domine.

HEAR the right, O Lord, confider my complaint : and hearken unto my prayer, that goeth not out of feigned lips.

2 Let my fentence come forth from thy prefence : and let thine eyes look upon the thing that is equal.

3 Thou haft proved and vifited mine heart in the night-feafon ; thou haft tried me, and fhalt find no wickednefs in me : for I am utterly purpofed that my mouth fhall not offend.

4 Becaufe of men's works, that are done againft the words of thy lips : I have kept me from the ways of the deftroyer.

5 O hold thou up my goings in thy paths : that my footfteps flip not.

6 I have called upon thee, O God, for thou fhalt hear me : incline thine ear to me, and hearken unto my words.

7 Shew thy marvellous loving-kindnefs, thou that art the Saviour of them which put their truft in thee : from fuch as refift thy right hand.

8 Keep me as the apple of an eye : hide me under the fhadow of thy wings,

9 From the ungodly that trouble me : mine enemies compafs me round about to take away my foul.

10 They are inclofed in their own fat : and their mouth fpeaketh proud things.

11 They lie waiting in our way on every fide : turning their eyes down to the ground ;

12 Like as a lion that is greedy of his prey : and as it were a lion's whelp, lurking in fecret places.

13 Up, Lord, difappoint him, and caft him down : deliver my foul from the ungodly, which is a fword of thine ;

14 From the men of thy hand, O Lord, from the men, I fay, and from the evil world : which have their portion in this life, whofe bellies thou filleft with thy hid treafure.

15 They have children at their defire : and leave the reft of their fubftance for their babes.

16 But as for me, I will behold thy prefence in righteoufnefs : and when I awake up after thy likenefs, I fhall be fatisfied with it.

EVENING PRAYER

PSALM XVIII.

DILIGAM TE DOMINE

I WILL love thee, O Lord, my ftrength ; the Lord is my ftony rock, and my defence : my Saviour, my God, and my might, in whom I will truft, my buckler, the horn alfo of my falvation, and my refuge.

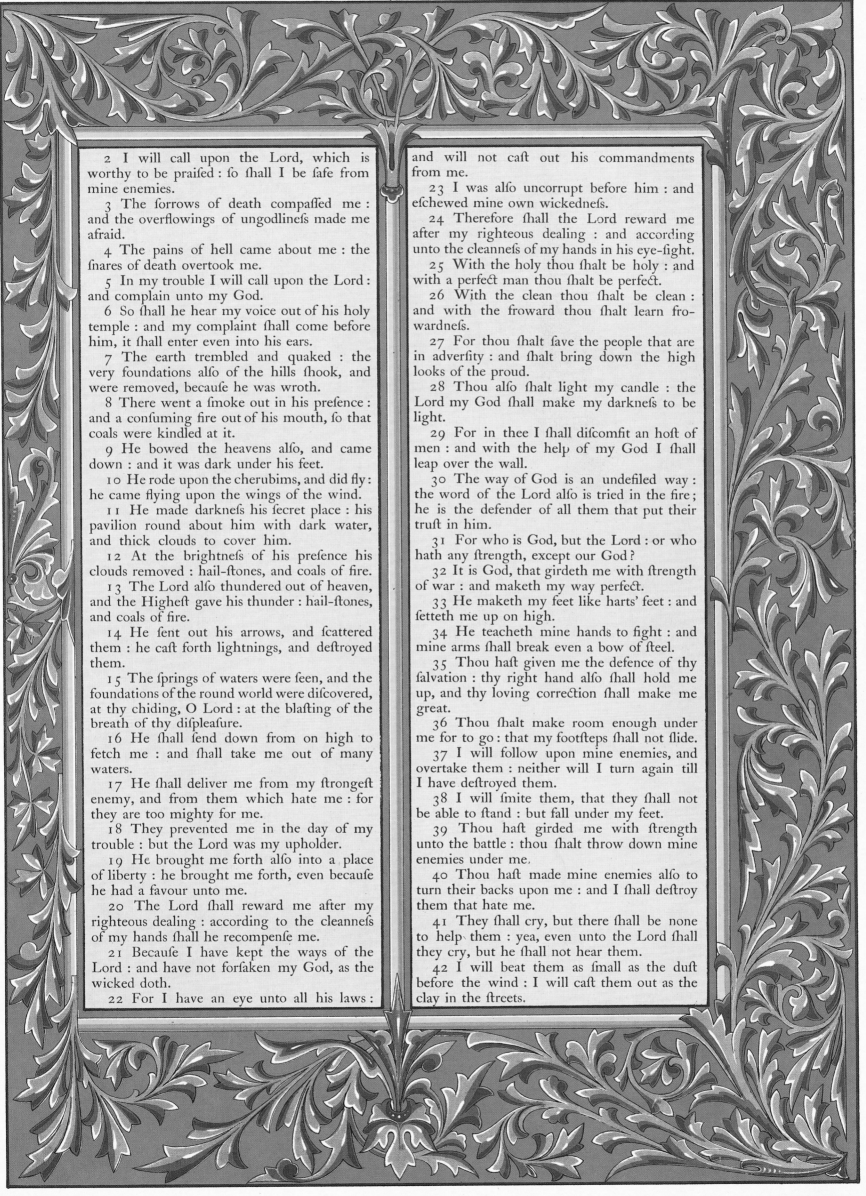

2 I will call upon the Lord, which is worthy to be praifed : fo fhall I be fafe from mine enemies.

3 The forrows of death compaffed me : and the overflowings of ungodlinefs made me afraid.

4 The pains of hell came about me : the fnares of death overtook me.

5 In my trouble I will call upon the Lord : and complain unto my God.

6 So fhall he hear my voice out of his holy temple : and my complaint fhall come before him, it fhall enter even into his ears.

7 The earth trembled and quaked : the very foundations alfo of the hills fhook, and were removed, becaufe he was wroth.

8 There went a fmoke out in his prefence : and a confuming fire out of his mouth, fo that coals were kindled at it.

9 He bowed the heavens alfo, and came down : and it was dark under his feet.

10 He rode upon the cherubims, and did fly : he came flying upon the wings of the wind.

11 He made darknefs his fecret place : his pavilion round about him with dark water, and thick clouds to cover him.

12 At the brightnefs of his prefence his clouds removed : hail-ftones, and coals of fire.

13 The Lord alfo thundered out of heaven, and the Higheft gave his thunder : hail-ftones, and coals of fire.

14 He fent out his arrows, and fcattered them : he caft forth lightnings, and deftroyed them.

15 The fprings of waters were feen, and the foundations of the round world were difcovered, at thy chiding, O Lord : at the blafting of the breath of thy difpleafure.

16 He fhall fend down from on high to fetch me : and fhall take me out of many waters.

17 He fhall deliver me from my ftrongeft enemy, and from them which hate me : for they are too mighty for me.

18 They prevented me in the day of my trouble : but the Lord was my upholder.

19 He brought me forth alfo into a place of liberty : he brought me forth, even becaufe he had a favour unto me.

20 The Lord fhall reward me after my righteous dealing : according to the cleannefs of my hands fhall he recompenfe me.

21 Becaufe I have kept the ways of the Lord : and have not forfaken my God, as the wicked doth.

22 For I have an eye unto all his laws : and will not caft out his commandments from me.

23 I was alfo uncorrupt before him : and efchewed mine own wickednefs.

24 Therefore fhall the Lord reward me after my righteous dealing : and according unto the cleannefs of my hands in his eye-fight.

25 With the holy thou fhalt be holy : and with a perfect man thou fhalt be perfect.

26 With the clean thou fhalt be clean : and with the froward thou fhalt learn frowardnefs.

27 For thou fhalt fave the people that are in adverfity : and fhalt bring down the high looks of the proud.

28 Thou alfo fhalt light my candle : the Lord my God fhall make my darknefs to be light.

29 For in thee I fhall difcomfit an hoft of men : and with the help of my God I fhall leap over the wall.

30 The way of God is an undefiled way : the word of the Lord alfo is tried in the fire ; he is the defender of all them that put their truft in him.

31 For who is God, but the Lord : or who hath any ftrength, except our God ?

32 It is God, that girdeth me with ftrength of war : and maketh my way perfect.

33 He maketh my feet like harts' feet : and fetteth me up on high.

34 He teacheth mine hands to fight : and mine arms fhall break even a bow of fteel.

35 Thou haft given me the defence of thy falvation : thy right hand alfo fhall hold me up, and thy loving correction fhall make me great.

36 Thou fhalt make room enough under me for to go : that my footfteps fhall not flide.

37 I will follow upon mine enemies, and overtake them : neither will I turn again till I have deftroyed them.

38 I will fmite them, that they fhall not be able to ftand : but fall under my feet.

39 Thou haft girded me with ftrength unto the battle : thou fhalt throw down mine enemies under me.

40 Thou haft made mine enemies alfo to turn their backs upon me : and I fhall deftroy them that hate me.

41 They fhall cry, but there fhall be none to help them : yea, even unto the Lord fhall they cry, but he fhall not hear them.

42 I will beat them as fmall as the duft before the wind : I will caft them out as the clay in the ftreets.

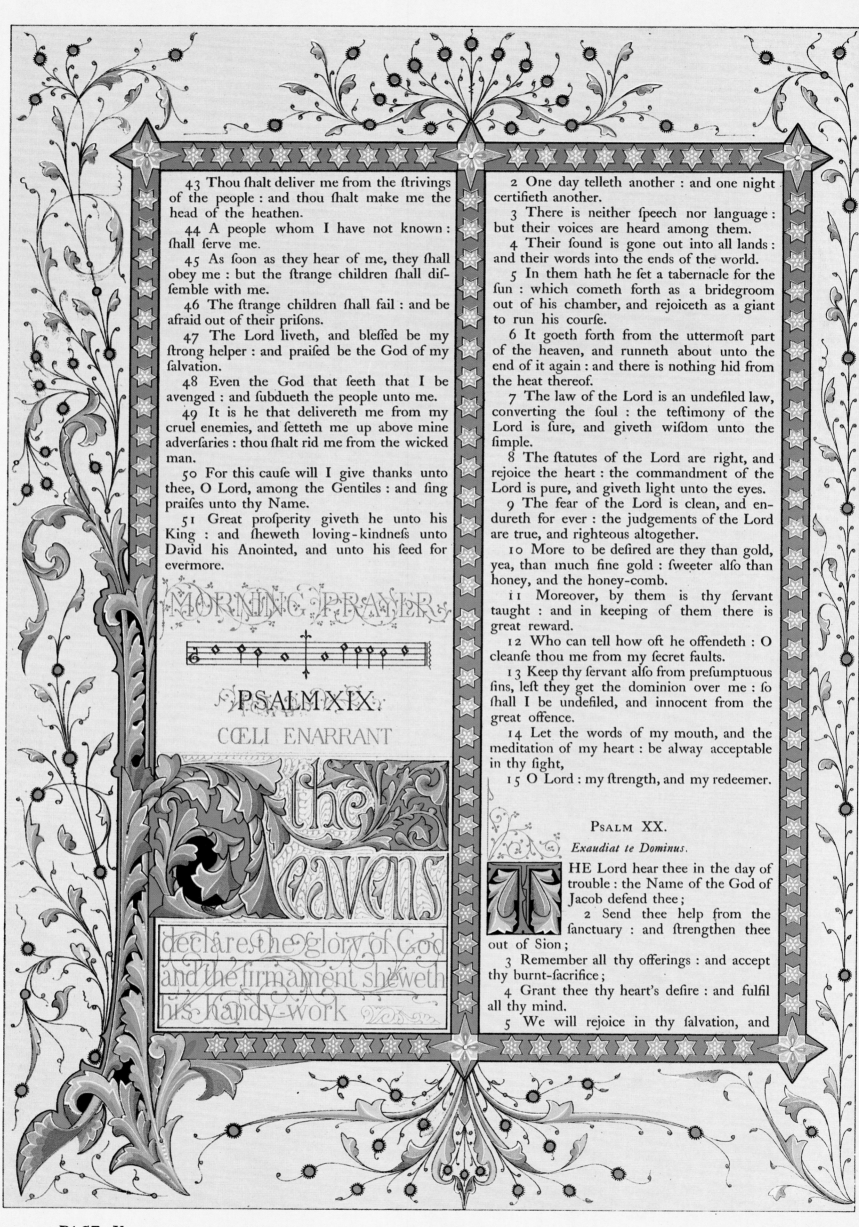

43 Thou shalt deliver me from the strivings of the people : and thou shalt make me the head of the heathen.

44 A people whom I have not known : shall serve me.

45 As soon as they hear of me, they shall obey me : but the strange children shall dissemble with me.

46 The strange children shall fail : and be afraid out of their prisons.

47 The Lord liveth, and blessed be my strong helper : and praised be the God of my salvation.

48 Even the God that seeth that I be avenged : and subdueth the people unto me.

49 It is he that delivereth me from my cruel enemies, and setteth me up above mine adversaries : thou shalt rid me from the wicked man.

50 For this cause will I give thanks unto thee, O Lord, among the Gentiles : and sing praises unto thy Name.

51 Great prosperity giveth he unto his King : and sheweth loving-kindness unto David his Anointed, and unto his seed for evermore.

MORNING PRAYER

PSALM XIX.

CŒLI ENARRANT

the Heavens declare the glory of God and the firmament sheweth his handy-work

2 One day telleth another : and one night certifieth another.

3 There is neither speech nor language : but their voices are heard among them.

4 Their sound is gone out into all lands : and their words into the ends of the world.

5 In them hath he set a tabernacle for the sun : which cometh forth as a bridegroom out of his chamber, and rejoiceth as a giant to run his course.

6 It goeth forth from the uttermost part of the heaven, and runneth about unto the end of it again : and there is nothing hid from the heat thereof.

7 The law of the Lord is an undefiled law, converting the soul : the testimony of the Lord is sure, and giveth wisdom unto the simple.

8 The statutes of the Lord are right, and rejoice the heart : the commandment of the Lord is pure, and giveth light unto the eyes.

9 The fear of the Lord is clean, and endureth for ever : the judgements of the Lord are true, and righteous altogether.

10 More to be desired are they than gold, yea, than much fine gold : sweeter also than honey, and the honey-comb.

11 Moreover, by them is thy servant taught : and in keeping of them there is great reward.

12 Who can tell how oft he offendeth : O cleanse thou me from my secret faults.

13 Keep thy servant also from presumptuous sins, lest they get the dominion over me : so shall I be undefiled, and innocent from the great offence.

14 Let the words of my mouth, and the meditation of my heart : be alway acceptable in thy sight,

15 O Lord : my strength, and my redeemer.

Psalm XX.

Exaudiat te Dominus.

THE Lord hear thee in the day of trouble : the Name of the God of Jacob defend thee;

2 Send thee help from the sanctuary : and strengthen thee out of Sion;

3 Remember all thy offerings : and accept thy burnt-sacrifice;

4 Grant thee thy heart's desire : and fulfil all thy mind.

5 We will rejoice in thy salvation, and

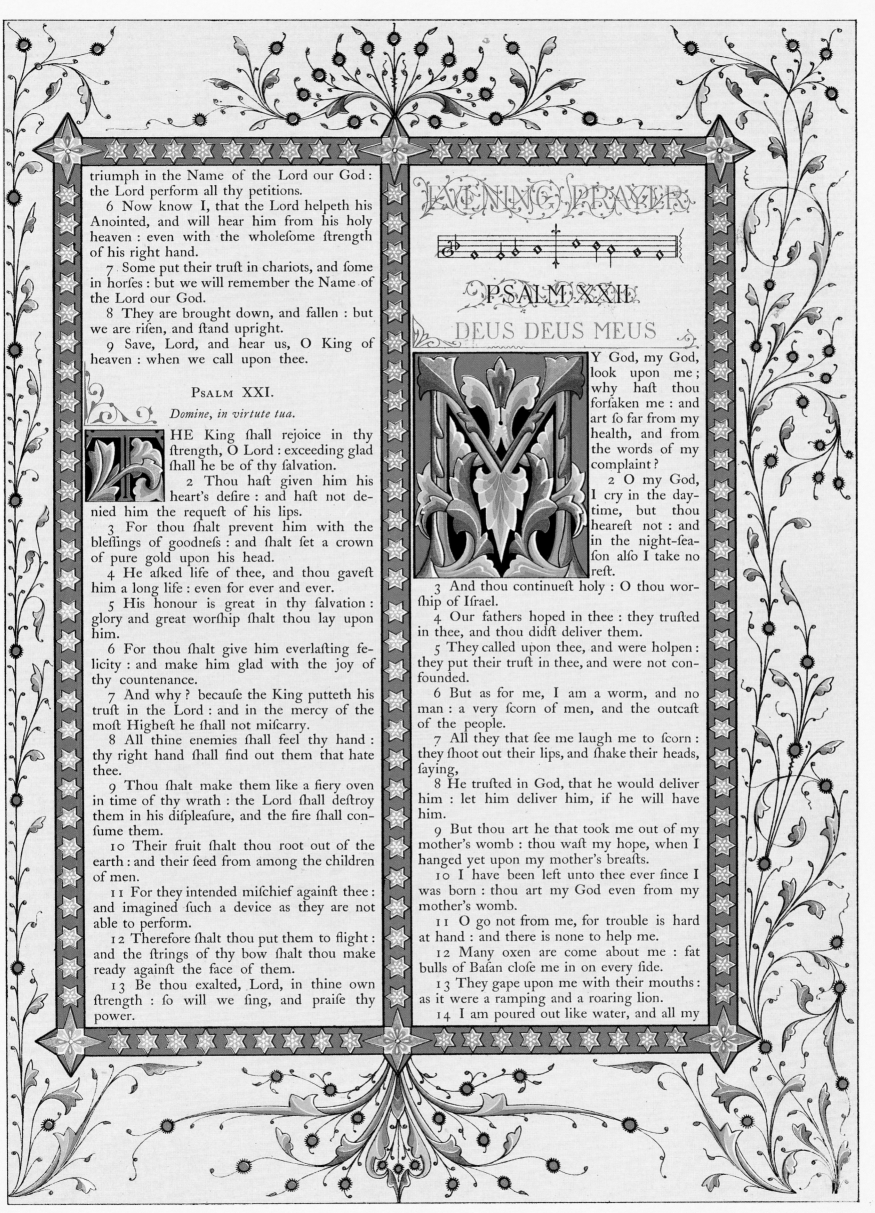

triumph in the Name of the Lord our God : the Lord perform all thy petitions.

6 Now know I, that the Lord helpeth his Anointed, and will hear him from his holy heaven : even with the wholeſome ſtrength of his right hand.

7 Some put their truſt in chariots, and ſome in horſes : but we will remember the Name of the Lord our God.

8 They are brought down, and fallen : but we are riſen, and ſtand upright.

9 Save, Lord, and hear us, O King of heaven : when we call upon thee.

PSALM XXI.

Domine, in virtute tua.

THE King ſhall rejoice in thy ſtrength, O Lord : exceeding glad ſhall he be of thy ſalvation.

2 Thou haſt given him his heart's deſire : and haſt not denied him the requeſt of his lips.

3 For thou ſhalt prevent him with the bleſſings of goodneſs : and ſhalt ſet a crown of pure gold upon his head.

4 He aſked life of thee, and thou gaveſt him a long life : even for ever and ever.

5 His honour is great in thy ſalvation : glory and great worſhip ſhalt thou lay upon him.

6 For thou ſhalt give him everlaſting felicity : and make him glad with the joy of thy countenance.

7 And why ? becauſe the King putteth his truſt in the Lord : and in the mercy of the moſt Higheſt he ſhall not miſcarry.

8 All thine enemies ſhall feel thy hand : thy right hand ſhall find out them that hate thee.

9 Thou ſhalt make them like a fiery oven in time of thy wrath : the Lord ſhall deſtroy them in his diſpleaſure, and the fire ſhall conſume them.

10 Their fruit ſhalt thou root out of the earth : and their ſeed from among the children of men.

11 For they intended miſchief againſt thee : and imagined ſuch a device as they are not able to perform.

12 Therefore ſhalt thou put them to flight : and the ſtrings of thy bow ſhalt thou make ready againſt the face of them.

13 Be thou exalted, Lord, in thine own ſtrength : ſo will we ſing, and praiſe thy power.

EVENING PRAYER.

PSALM XXII.
DEUS DEUS MEUS

MY God, my God, look upon me ; why haſt thou forſaken me : and art ſo far from my health, and from the words of my complaint ?

2 O my God, I cry in the day-time, but thou heareſt not : and in the night-ſeaſon alſo I take no reſt.

3 And thou continueſt holy : O thou worſhip of Iſrael.

4 Our fathers hoped in thee : they truſted in thee, and thou didſt deliver them.

5 They called upon thee, and were holpen : they put their truſt in thee, and were not confounded.

6 But as for me, I am a worm, and no man : a very ſcorn of men, and the outcaſt of the people.

7 All they that ſee me laugh me to ſcorn : they ſhoot out their lips, and ſhake their heads, ſaying,

8 He truſted in God, that he would deliver him : let him deliver him, if he will have him.

9 But thou art he that took me out of my mother's womb : thou waſt my hope, when I hanged yet upon my mother's breaſts.

10 I have been left unto thee ever ſince I was born : thou art my God even from my mother's womb.

11 O go not from me, for trouble is hard at hand : and there is none to help me.

12 Many oxen are come about me : fat bulls of Baſan cloſe me in on every ſide.

13 They gape upon me with their mouths : as it were a ramping and a roaring lion.

14 I am poured out like water, and all my

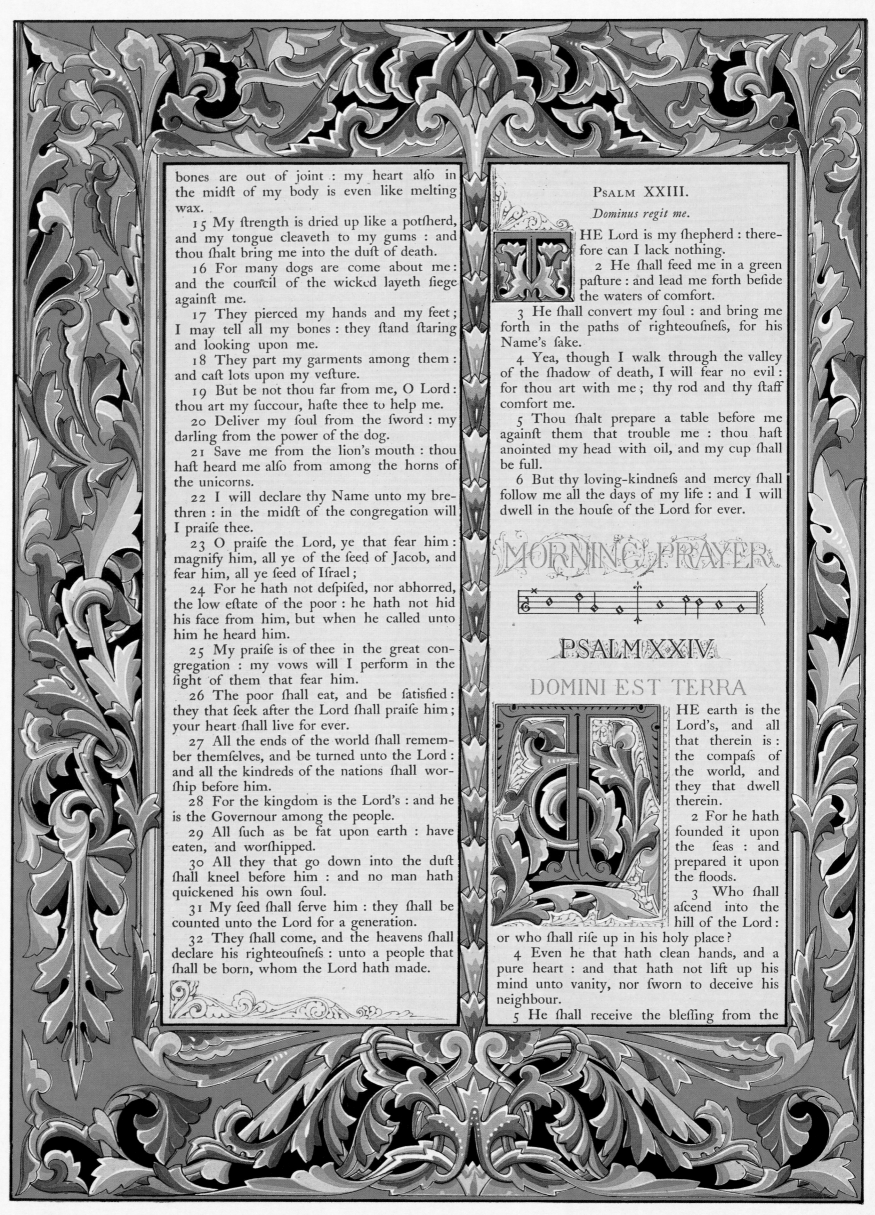

bones are out of joint : my heart also in the midst of my body is even like melting wax.

15 My strength is dried up like a potsherd, and my tongue cleaveth to my gums : and thou shalt bring me into the dust of death.

16 For many dogs are come about me : and the council of the wicked layeth siege against me.

17 They pierced my hands and my feet ; I may tell all my bones : they stand staring and looking upon me.

18 They part my garments among them : and cast lots upon my vesture.

19 But be not thou far from me, O Lord : thou art my succour, haste thee to help me.

20 Deliver my soul from the sword : my darling from the power of the dog.

21 Save me from the lion's mouth : thou hast heard me also from among the horns of the unicorns.

22 I will declare thy Name unto my brethren : in the midst of the congregation will I praise thee.

23 O praise the Lord, ye that fear him : magnify him, all ye of the seed of Jacob, and fear him, all ye seed of Israel ;

24 For he hath not despised, nor abhorred, the low estate of the poor : he hath not hid his face from him, but when he called unto him he heard him.

25 My praise is of thee in the great congregation : my vows will I perform in the sight of them that fear him.

26 The poor shall eat, and be satisfied : they that seek after the Lord shall praise him ; your heart shall live for ever.

27 All the ends of the world shall remember themselves, and be turned unto the Lord : and all the kindreds of the nations shall worship before him.

28 For the kingdom is the Lord's : and he is the Governour among the people.

29 All such as be fat upon earth : have eaten, and worshipped.

30 All they that go down into the dust shall kneel before him : and no man hath quickened his own soul.

31 My seed shall serve him : they shall be counted unto the Lord for a generation.

32 They shall come, and the heavens shall declare his righteousness : unto a people that shall be born, whom the Lord hath made.

Psalm XXIII.

Dominus regit me.

THE Lord is my shepherd : therefore can I lack nothing.

2 He shall feed me in a green pasture : and lead me forth beside the waters of comfort.

3 He shall convert my soul : and bring me forth in the paths of righteousness, for his Name's sake.

4 Yea, though I walk through the valley of the shadow of death, I will fear no evil : for thou art with me ; thy rod and thy staff comfort me.

5 Thou shalt prepare a table before me against them that trouble me : thou hast anointed my head with oil, and my cup shall be full.

6 But thy loving-kindness and mercy shall follow me all the days of my life : and I will dwell in the house of the Lord for ever.

MORNING PRAYER

PSALM XXIV

DOMINI EST TERRA

THE earth is the Lord's, and all that therein is : the compass of the world, and they that dwell therein.

2 For he hath founded it upon the seas : and prepared it upon the floods.

3 Who shall ascend into the hill of the Lord : or who shall rise up in his holy place ?

4 Even he that hath clean hands, and a pure heart : and that hath not lift up his mind unto vanity, nor sworn to deceive his neighbour.

5 He shall receive the blessing from the

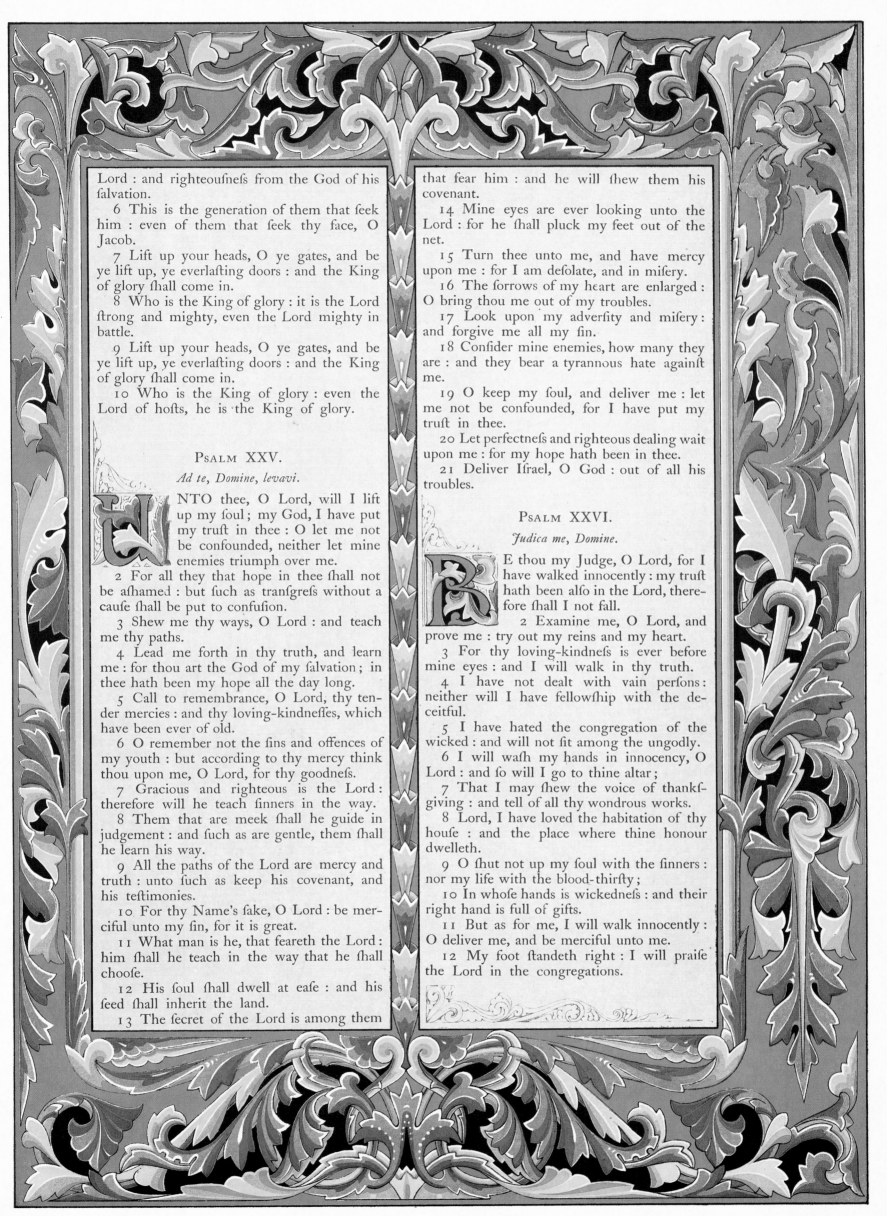

Lord : and righteousnefs from the God of his falvation.

6 This is the generation of them that feek him : even of them that feek thy face, O Jacob.

7 Lift up your heads, O ye gates, and be ye lift up, ye everlasting doors : and the King of glory shall come in.

8 Who is the King of glory : it is the Lord strong and mighty, even the Lord mighty in battle.

9 Lift up your heads, O ye gates, and be ye lift up, ye everlasting doors : and the King of glory shall come in.

10 Who is the King of glory : even the Lord of hofts, he is the King of glory.

Psalm XXV.

Ad te, Domine, levavi.

UNTO thee, O Lord, will I lift up my foul; my God, I have put my truft in thee : O let me not be confounded, neither let mine enemies triumph over me.

2 For all they that hope in thee shall not be ashamed : but such as transgrefs without a caufe shall be put to confusion.

3 Shew me thy ways, O Lord : and teach me thy paths.

4 Lead me forth in thy truth, and learn me : for thou art the God of my falvation; in thee hath been my hope all the day long.

5 Call to remembrance, O Lord, thy tender mercies : and thy loving-kindneffes, which have been ever of old.

6 O remember not the fins and offences of my youth : but according to thy mercy think thou upon me, O Lord, for thy goodnefs.

7 Gracious and righteous is the Lord : therefore will he teach finners in the way.

8 Them that are meek shall he guide in judgement : and such as are gentle, them shall he learn his way.

9 All the paths of the Lord are mercy and truth : unto such as keep his covenant, and his testimonies.

10 For thy Name's fake, O Lord : be merciful unto my fin, for it is great.

11 What man is he, that feareth the Lord : him shall he teach in the way that he shall choose.

12 His foul shall dwell at eafe : and his feed shall inherit the land.

13 The fecret of the Lord is among them

that fear him : and he will shew them his covenant.

14 Mine eyes are ever looking unto the Lord : for he shall pluck my feet out of the net.

15 Turn thee unto me, and have mercy upon me : for I am defolate, and in mifery.

16 The forrows of my heart are enlarged : O bring thou me out of my troubles.

17 Look upon my adverfity and mifery : and forgive me all my fin.

18 Confider mine enemies, how many they are : and they bear a tyrannous hate againft me.

19 O keep my foul, and deliver me : let me not be confounded, for I have put my truft in thee.

20 Let perfectnefs and righteous dealing wait upon me : for my hope hath been in thee.

21 Deliver Ifrael, O God : out of all his troubles.

Psalm XXVI.

Judica me, Domine.

BE thou my Judge, O Lord, for I have walked innocently : my truft hath been alfo in the Lord, therefore shall I not fall.

2 Examine me, O Lord, and prove me : try out my reins and my heart.

3 For thy loving-kindnefs is ever before mine eyes : and I will walk in thy truth.

4 I have not dealt with vain perfons : neither will I have fellowship with the deceitful.

5 I have hated the congregation of the wicked : and will not fit among the ungodly.

6 I will wash my hands in innocency, O Lord : and fo will I go to thine altar;

7 That I may shew the voice of thankfgiving : and tell of all thy wondrous works.

8 Lord, I have loved the habitation of thy houfe : and the place where thine honour dwelleth.

9 O shut not up my foul with the finners : nor my life with the blood-thirfty;

10 In whofe hands is wickednefs : and their right hand is full of gifts.

11 But as for me, I will walk innocently : O deliver me, and be merciful unto me.

12 My foot ftandeth right : I will praife the Lord in the congregations.

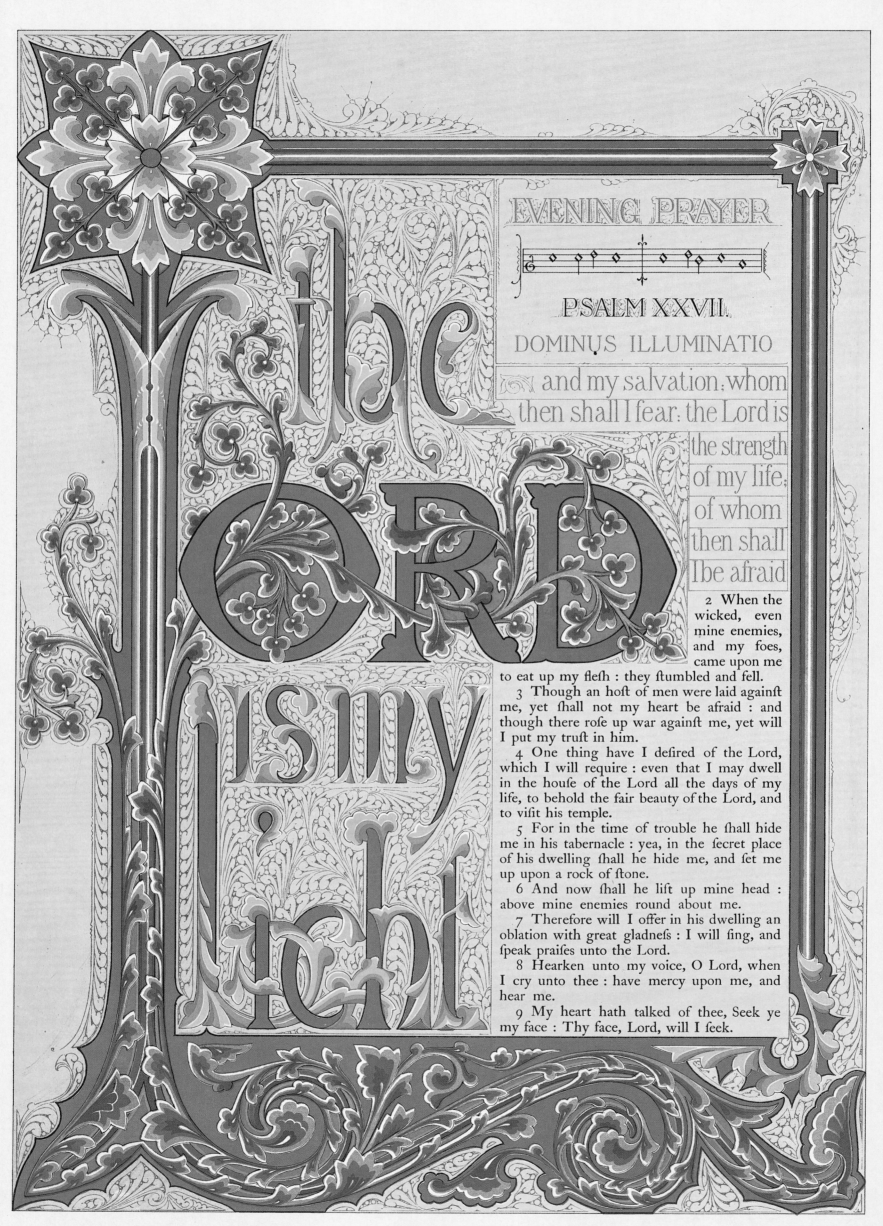

EVENING PRAYER

PSALM XXVII.

DOMINUS ILLUMINATIO

and my salvation: whom then shall I fear: the Lord is the strength of my life; of whom then shall I be afraid

2 When the wicked, even mine enemies, and my foes, came upon me to eat up my fleſh : they ſtumbled and fell.

3 Though an hoſt of men were laid againſt me, yet ſhall not my heart be afraid : and though there roſe up war againſt me, yet will I put my truſt in him.

4 One thing have I deſired of the Lord, which I will require : even that I may dwell in the houſe of the Lord all the days of my life, to behold the fair beauty of the Lord, and to viſit his temple.

5 For in the time of trouble he ſhall hide me in his tabernacle : yea, in the ſecret place of his dwelling ſhall he hide me, and ſet me up upon a rock of ſtone.

6 And now ſhall he lift up mine head : above mine enemies round about me.

7 Therefore will I offer in his dwelling an oblation with great gladneſs : I will ſing, and ſpeak praiſes unto the Lord.

8 Hearken unto my voice, O Lord, when I cry unto thee : have mercy upon me, and hear me.

9 My heart hath talked of thee, Seek ye my face : Thy face, Lord, will I ſeek.

the LORD is my Light

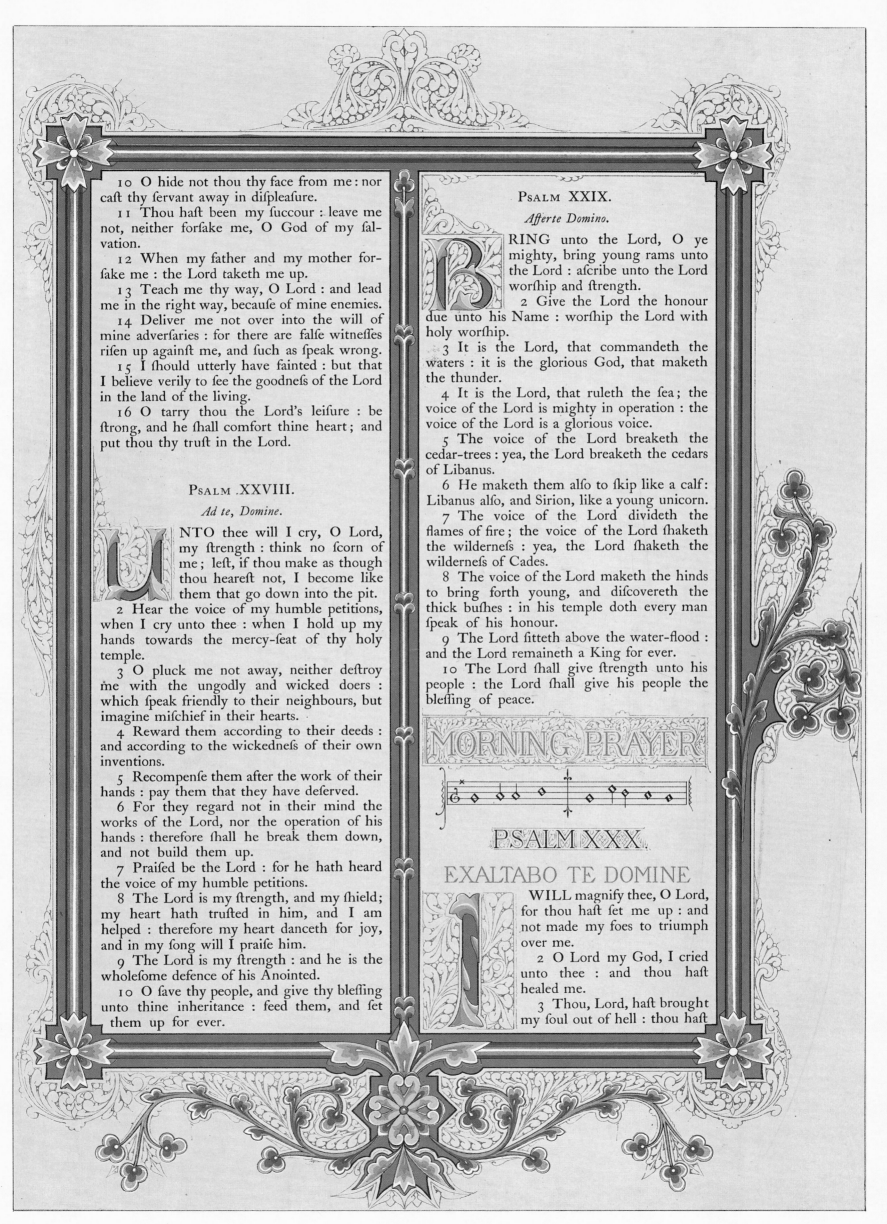

10 O hide not thou thy face from me : nor caſt thy ſervant away in diſpleaſure.

11 Thou haſt been my ſuccour : leave me not, neither forſake me, O God of my ſalvation.

12 When my father and my mother forſake me : the Lord taketh me up.

13 Teach me thy way, O Lord : and lead me in the right way, becauſe of mine enemies.

14 Deliver me not over into the will of mine adverſaries : for there are falſe witneſſes riſen up againſt me, and ſuch as ſpeak wrong.

15 I ſhould utterly have fainted : but that I believe verily to ſee the goodneſs of the Lord in the land of the living.

16 O tarry thou the Lord's leiſure : be ſtrong, and he ſhall comfort thine heart; and put thou thy truſt in the Lord.

Psalm .XXVIII.

Ad te, Domine.

UNTO thee will I cry, O Lord, my ſtrength : think no ſcorn of me; leſt, if thou make as though thou heareſt not, I become like them that go down into the pit.

2 Hear the voice of my humble petitions, when I cry unto thee : when I hold up my hands towards the mercy-ſeat of thy holy temple.

3 O pluck me not away, neither deſtroy me with the ungodly and wicked doers : which ſpeak friendly to their neighbours, but imagine miſchief in their hearts.

4 Reward them according to their deeds : and according to the wickedneſs of their own inventions.

5 Recompenſe them after the work of their hands : pay them that they have deſerved.

6 For they regard not in their mind the works of the Lord, nor the operation of his hands : therefore ſhall he break them down, and not build them up.

7 Praiſed be the Lord : for he hath heard the voice of my humble petitions.

8 The Lord is my ſtrength, and my ſhield; my heart hath truſted in him, and I am helped : therefore my heart danceth for joy, and in my ſong will I praiſe him.

9 The Lord is my ſtrength : and he is the wholeſome defence of his Anointed.

10 O ſave thy people, and give thy bleſſing unto thine inheritance : feed them, and ſet them up for ever.

Psalm XXIX.

Afferte Domino.

BRING unto the Lord, O ye mighty, bring young rams unto the Lord : aſcribe unto the Lord worſhip and ſtrength.

2 Give the Lord the honour due unto his Name : worſhip the Lord with holy worſhip.

3 It is the Lord, that commandeth the waters : it is the glorious God, that maketh the thunder.

4 It is the Lord, that ruleth the ſea; the voice of the Lord is mighty in operation : the voice of the Lord is a glorious voice.

5 The voice of the Lord breaketh the cedar-trees : yea, the Lord breaketh the cedars of Libanus.

6 He maketh them alſo to ſkip like a calf : Libanus alſo, and Sirion, like a young unicorn.

7 The voice of the Lord divideth the flames of fire ; the voice of the Lord ſhaketh the wilderneſs : yea, the Lord ſhaketh the wilderneſs of Cades.

8 The voice of the Lord maketh the hinds to bring forth young, and diſcovereth the thick buſhes : in his temple doth every man ſpeak of his honour.

9 The Lord ſitteth above the water-flood : and the Lord remaineth a King for ever.

10 The Lord ſhall give ſtrength unto his people : the Lord ſhall give his people the bleſſing of peace.

MORNING PRAYER

PSALM XXX.

EXALTABO TE DOMINE

I WILL magnify thee, O Lord, for thou haſt ſet me up : and not made my foes to triumph over me.

2 O Lord my God, I cried unto thee : and thou haſt healed me.

3 Thou, Lord, haſt brought my ſoul out of hell : thou haſt

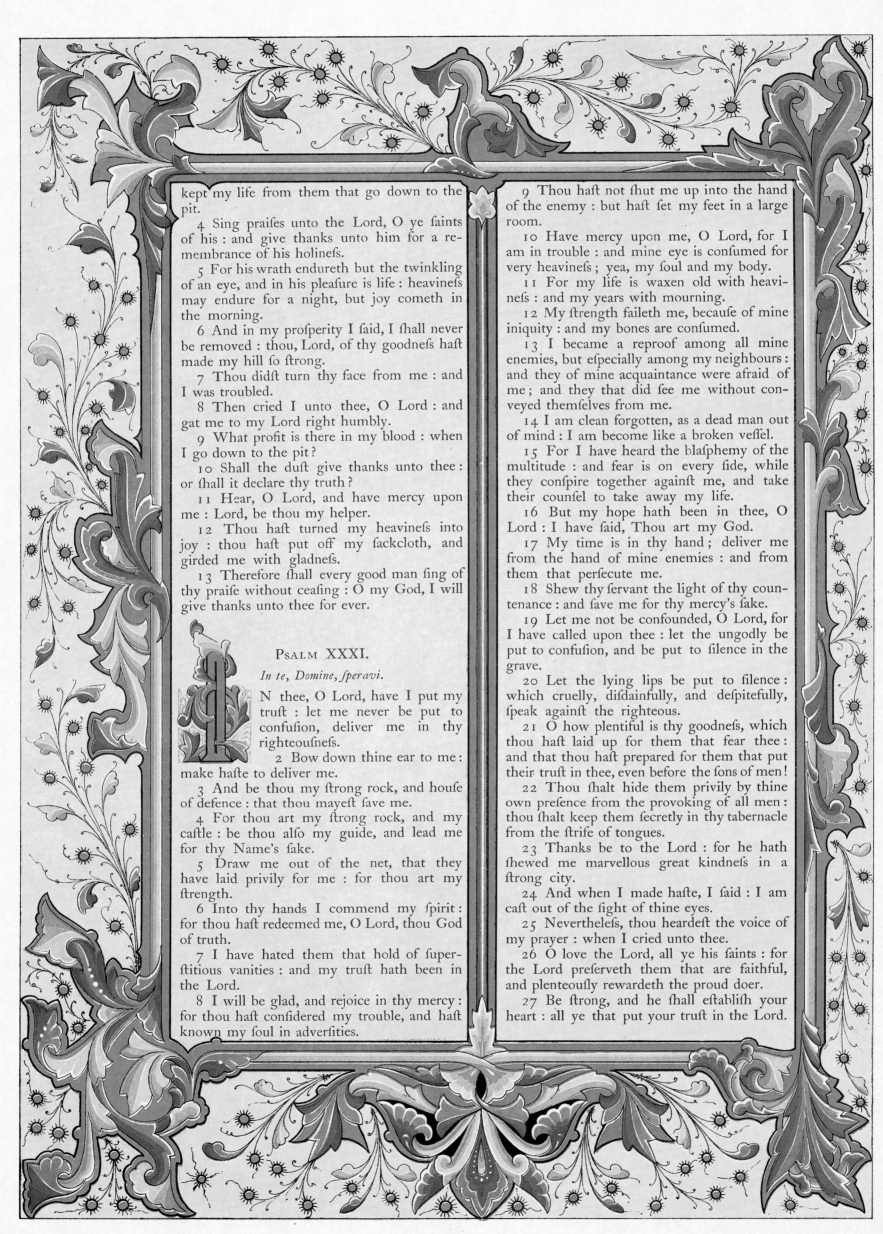

kept my life from them that go down to the pit.

4 Sing praifes unto the Lord, O ye faints of his : and give thanks unto him for a remembrance of his holinefs.

5 For his wrath endureth but the twinkling of an eye, and in his pleafure is life : heavinefs may endure for a night, but joy cometh in the morning.

6 And in my profperity I faid, I fhall never be removed : thou, Lord, of thy goodnefs haft made my hill fo ftrong.

7 Thou didft turn thy face from me : and I was troubled.

8 Then cried I unto thee, O Lord : and gat me to my Lord right humbly.

9 What profit is there in my blood : when I go down to the pit?

10 Shall the duft give thanks unto thee : or fhall it declare thy truth?

11 Hear, O Lord, and have mercy upon me : Lord, be thou my helper.

12 Thou haft turned my heavinefs into joy : thou haft put off my fackcloth, and girded me with gladnefs.

13 Therefore fhall every good man fing of thy praife without ceafing : O my God, I will give thanks unto thee for ever.

Psalm XXXI.

In te, Domine, fperavi.

N thee, O Lord, have I put my truft : let me never be put to confufion, deliver me in thy righteoufnefs.

2 Bow down thine ear to me : make hafte to deliver me.

3 And be thou my ftrong rock, and houfe of defence : that thou mayeft fave me.

4 For thou art my ftrong rock, and my caftle : be thou alfo my guide, and lead me for thy Name's fake.

5 Draw me out of the net, that they have laid privily for me : for thou art my ftrength.

6 Into thy hands I commend my fpirit : for thou haft redeemed me, O Lord, thou God of truth.

7 I have hated them that hold of fuperftitious vanities : and my truft hath been in the Lord.

8 I will be glad, and rejoice in thy mercy : for thou haft confidered my trouble, and haft known my foul in adverfities.

9 Thou haft not fhut me up into the hand of the enemy : but haft fet my feet in a large room.

10 Have mercy upon me, O Lord, for I am in trouble : and mine eye is confumed for very heavinefs ; yea, my foul and my body.

11 For my life is waxen old with heavinefs : and my years with mourning.

12 My ftrength faileth me, becaufe of mine iniquity : and my bones are confumed.

13 I became a reproof among all mine enemies, but efpecially among my neighbours : and they of mine acquaintance were afraid of me ; and they that did fee me without conveyed themfelves from me.

14 I am clean forgotten, as a dead man out of mind : I am become like a broken veffel.

15 For I have heard the blafphemy of the multitude : and fear is on every fide, while they confpire together againft me, and take their counfel to take away my life.

16 But my hope hath been in thee, O Lord : I have faid, Thou art my God.

17 My time is in thy hand ; deliver me from the hand of mine enemies : and from them that perfecute me.

18 Shew thy fervant the light of thy countenance : and fave me for thy mercy's fake.

19 Let me not be confounded, O Lord, for I have called upon thee : let the ungodly be put to confufion, and be put to filence in the grave.

20 Let the lying lips be put to filence : which cruelly, difdainfully, and defpitefully, fpeak againft the righteous.

21 O how plentiful is thy goodnefs, which thou haft laid up for them that fear thee : and that thou haft prepared for them that put their truft in thee, even before the fons of men !

22 Thou fhalt hide them privily by thine own prefence from the provoking of all men : thou fhalt keep them fecretly in thy tabernacle from the ftrife of tongues.

23 Thanks be to the Lord : for he hath fhewed me marvellous great kindnefs in a ftrong city.

24 And when I made hafte, I faid : I am caft out of the fight of thine eyes.

25 Neverthelefs, thou heardeft the voice of my prayer : when I cried unto thee.

26 O love the Lord, all ye his faints : for the Lord preferveth them that are faithful, and plenteoufly rewardeth the proud doer.

27 Be ftrong, and he fhall eftablifh your heart : all ye that put your truft in the Lord.

EVENING PRAYER

PSALM XXXII.

BEATI QUORUM

Bessed is he whose un-righteousness is forgiven and whose sin is covered

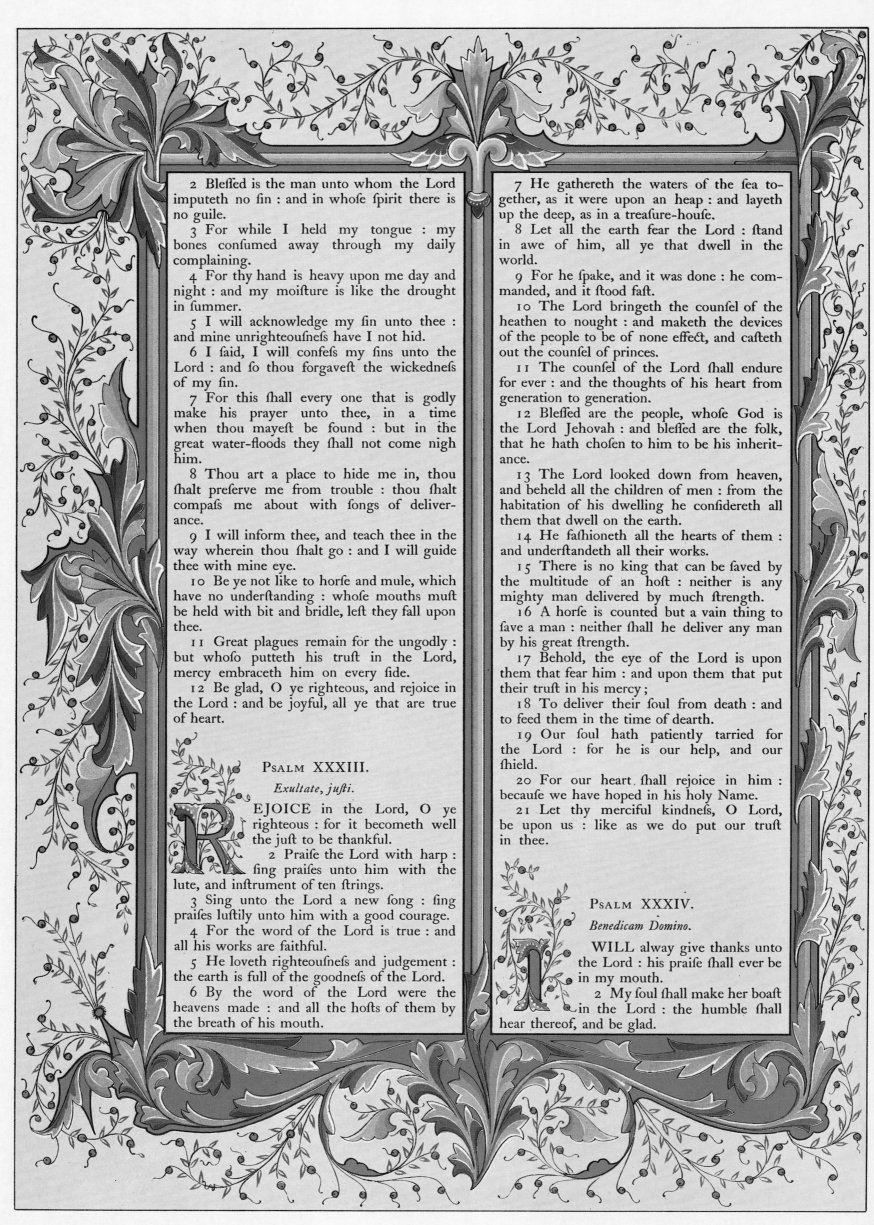

2 Blessed is the man unto whom the Lord imputeth no sin : and in whose spirit there is no guile.

3 For while I held my tongue : my bones consumed away through my daily complaining.

4 For thy hand is heavy upon me day and night : and my moisture is like the drought in summer.

5 I will acknowledge my sin unto thee : and mine unrighteousness have I not hid.

6 I said, I will confess my sins unto the Lord : and so thou forgavest the wickedness of my sin.

7 For this shall every one that is godly make his prayer unto thee, in a time when thou mayest be found : but in the great water-floods they shall not come nigh him.

8 Thou art a place to hide me in, thou shalt preserve me from trouble : thou shalt compass me about with songs of deliverance.

9 I will inform thee, and teach thee in the way wherein thou shalt go : and I will guide thee with mine eye.

10 Be ye not like to horse and mule, which have no understanding : whose mouths must be held with bit and bridle, lest they fall upon thee.

11 Great plagues remain for the ungodly : but whoso putteth his trust in the Lord, mercy embraceth him on every side.

12 Be glad, O ye righteous, and rejoice in the Lord : and be joyful, all ye that are true of heart.

PSALM XXXIII.

Exultate, justi.

REJOICE in the Lord, O ye righteous : for it becometh well the just to be thankful.

2 Praise the Lord with harp : sing praises unto him with the lute, and instrument of ten strings.

3 Sing unto the Lord a new song : sing praises lustily unto him with a good courage.

4 For the word of the Lord is true : and all his works are faithful.

5 He loveth righteousness and judgement : the earth is full of the goodness of the Lord.

6 By the word of the Lord were the heavens made : and all the hosts of them by the breath of his mouth.

7 He gathereth the waters of the sea together, as it were upon an heap : and layeth up the deep, as in a treasure-house.

8 Let all the earth fear the Lord : stand in awe of him, all ye that dwell in the world.

9 For he spake, and it was done : he commanded, and it stood fast.

10 The Lord bringeth the counsel of the heathen to nought : and maketh the devices of the people to be of none effect, and casteth out the counsel of princes.

11 The counsel of the Lord shall endure for ever : and the thoughts of his heart from generation to generation.

12 Blessed are the people, whose God is the Lord Jehovah : and blessed are the folk, that he hath chosen to him to be his inheritance.

13 The Lord looked down from heaven, and beheld all the children of men : from the habitation of his dwelling he considereth all them that dwell on the earth.

14 He fashioneth all the hearts of them : and understandeth all their works.

15 There is no king that can be saved by the multitude of an host : neither is any mighty man delivered by much strength.

16 A horse is counted but a vain thing to save a man : neither shall he deliver any man by his great strength.

17 Behold, the eye of the Lord is upon them that fear him : and upon them that put their trust in his mercy ;

18 To deliver their soul from death : and to feed them in the time of dearth.

19 Our soul hath patiently tarried for the Lord : for he is our help, and our shield.

20 For our heart shall rejoice in him : because we have hoped in his holy Name.

21 Let thy merciful kindness, O Lord, be upon us : like as we do put our trust in thee.

PSALM XXXIV.

Benedicam Domino.

I WILL alway give thanks unto the Lord : his praise shall ever be in my mouth.

2 My soul shall make her boast in the Lord : the humble shall hear thereof, and be glad.

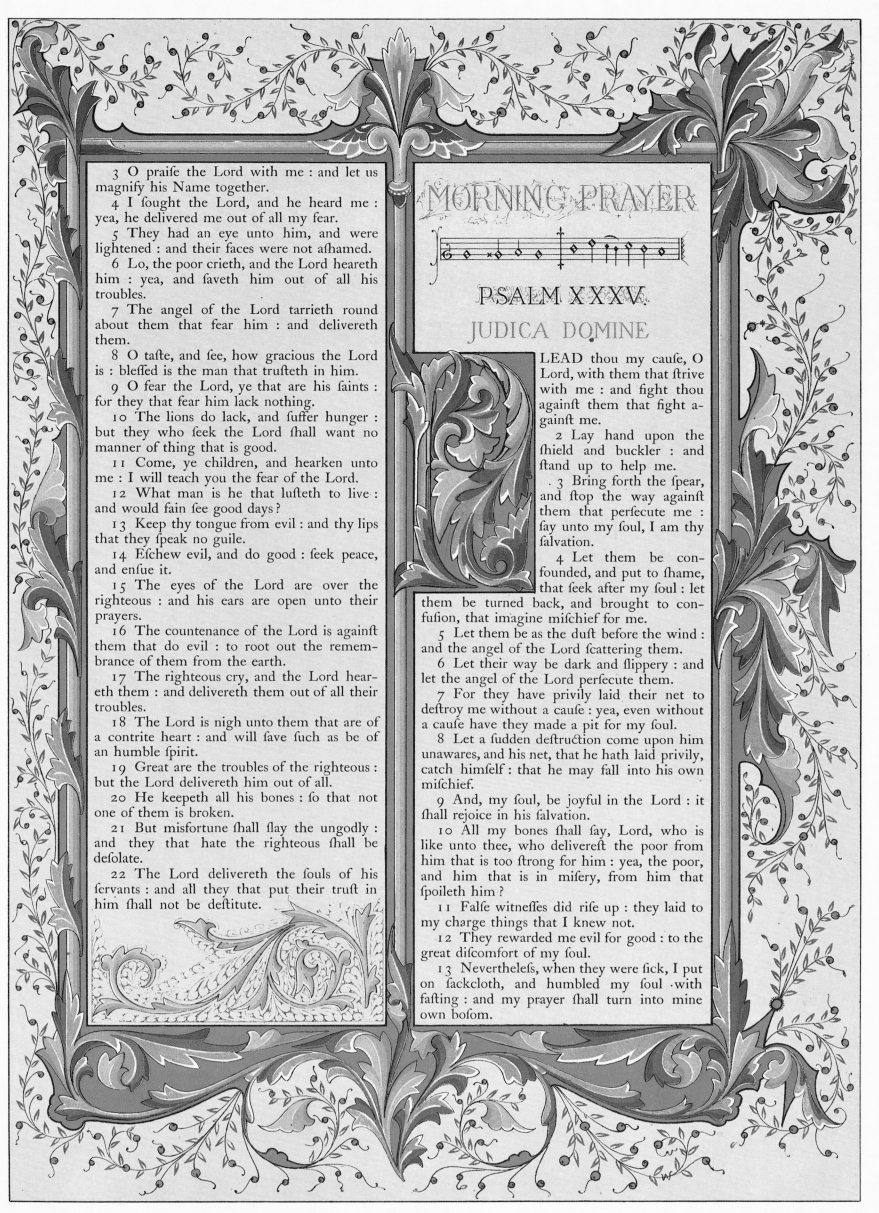

3 O praiſe the Lord with me : and let us magnify his Name together.

4 I ſought the Lord, and he heard me : yea, he delivered me out of all my fear.

5 They had an eye unto him, and were lightened : and their faces were not aſhamed.

6 Lo, the poor crieth, and the Lord heareth him : yea, and ſaveth him out of all his troubles.

7 The angel of the Lord tarrieth round about them that fear him : and delivereth them.

8 O taſte, and ſee, how gracious the Lord is : bleſſed is the man that truſteth in him.

9 O fear the Lord, ye that are his ſaints : for they that fear him lack nothing.

10 The lions do lack, and ſuffer hunger : but they who ſeek the Lord ſhall want no manner of thing that is good.

11 Come, ye children, and hearken unto me : I will teach you the fear of the Lord.

12 What man is he that luſteth to live : and would fain ſee good days ?

13 Keep thy tongue from evil : and thy lips that they ſpeak no guile.

14 Eſchew evil, and do good : ſeek peace, and enſue it.

15 The eyes of the Lord are over the righteous : and his ears are open unto their prayers.

16 The countenance of the Lord is againſt them that do evil : to root out the remembrance of them from the earth.

17 The righteous cry, and the Lord heareth them : and delivereth them out of all their troubles.

18 The Lord is nigh unto them that are of a contrite heart : and will ſave ſuch as be of an humble ſpirit.

19 Great are the troubles of the righteous : but the Lord delivereth him out of all.

20 He keepeth all his bones : ſo that not one of them is broken.

21 But misfortune ſhall ſlay the ungodly : and they that hate the righteous ſhall be deſolate.

22 The Lord delivereth the ſouls of his ſervants : and all they that put their truſt in him ſhall not be deſtitute.

MORNING PRAYER

PSALM XXXV.

JUDICA DOMINE

LEAD thou my cauſe, O Lord, with them that ſtrive with me : and fight thou againſt them that fight againſt me.

2 Lay hand upon the ſhield and buckler : and ſtand up to help me.

3 Bring forth the ſpear, and ſtop the way againſt them that perſecute me : ſay unto my ſoul, I am thy ſalvation.

4 Let them be confounded, and put to ſhame, that ſeek after my ſoul : let them be turned back, and brought to confuſion, that imagine miſchief for me.

5 Let them be as the duſt before the wind : and the angel of the Lord ſcattering them.

6 Let their way be dark and ſlippery : and let the angel of the Lord perſecute them.

7 For they have privily laid their net to deſtroy me without a cauſe : yea, even without a cauſe have they made a pit for my ſoul.

8 Let a ſudden deſtruction come upon him unawares, and his net, that he hath laid privily, catch himſelf : that he may fall into his own miſchief.

9 And, my ſoul, be joyful in the Lord : it ſhall rejoice in his ſalvation.

10 All my bones ſhall ſay, Lord, who is like unto thee, who delivereſt the poor from him that is too ſtrong for him : yea, the poor, and him that is in miſery, from him that ſpoileth him ?

11 Falſe witneſſes did riſe up : they laid to my charge things that I knew not.

12 They rewarded me evil for good : to the great diſcomfort of my ſoul.

13 Nevertheleſs, when they were ſick, I put on ſackcloth, and humbled my ſoul ·with faſting : and my prayer ſhall turn into mine own boſom.

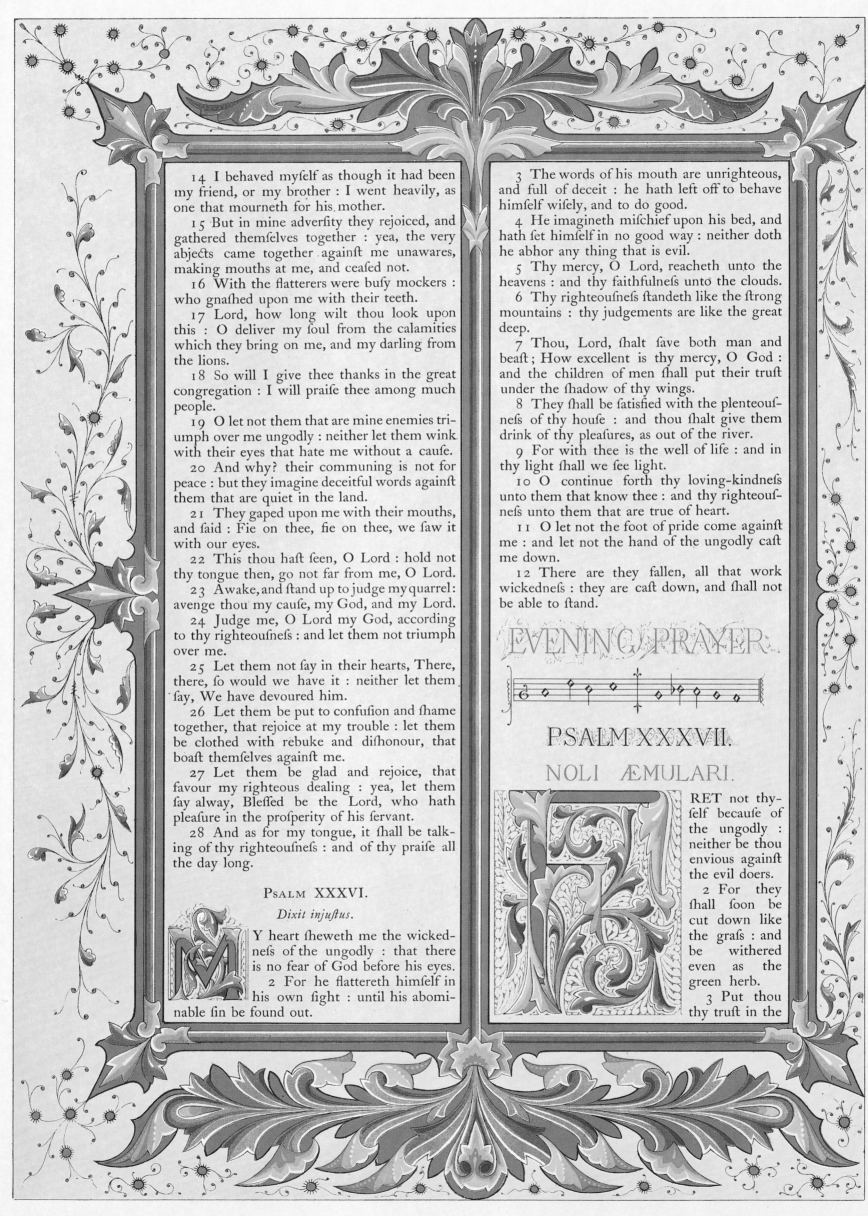

14 I behaved myself as though it had been my friend, or my brother : I went heavily, as one that mourneth for his mother.

15 But in mine adverfity they rejoiced, and gathered themfelves together : yea, the very abjects came together against me unawares, making mouths at me, and ceafed not.

16 With the flatterers were bufy mockers : who gnafhed upon me with their teeth.

17 Lord, how long wilt thou look upon this : O deliver my foul from the calamities which they bring on me, and my darling from the lions.

18 So will I give thee thanks in the great congregation : I will praife thee among much people.

19 O let not them that are mine enemies triumph over me ungodly : neither let them wink with their eyes that hate me without a caufe.

20 And why? their communing is not for peace : but they imagine deceitful words against them that are quiet in the land.

21 They gaped upon me with their mouths, and faid : Fie on thee, fie on thee, we faw it with our eyes.

22 This thou haft feen, O Lord : hold not thy tongue then, go not far from me, O Lord.

23 Awake, and ftand up to judge my quarrel : avenge thou my caufe, my God, and my Lord.

24 Judge me, O Lord my God, according to thy righteoufnefs : and let them not triumph over me.

25 Let them not fay in their hearts, There, there, fo would we have it : neither let them fay, We have devoured him.

26 Let them be put to confufion and fhame together, that rejoice at my trouble : let them be clothed with rebuke and difhonour, that boaft themfelves against me.

27 Let them be glad and rejoice, that favour my righteous dealing : yea, let them fay alway, Bleffed be the Lord, who hath pleafure in the profperity of his fervant.

28 And as for my tongue, it fhall be talking of thy righteoufnefs : and of thy praife all the day long.

Psalm XXXVI.

Dixit injuftus.

Y heart fheweth me the wickednefs of the ungodly : that there is no fear of God before his eyes.

2 For he flattereth himfelf in his own fight : until his abominable fin be found out.

3 The words of his mouth are unrighteous, and full of deceit : he hath left off to behave himfelf wifely, and to do good.

4 He imagineth mifchief upon his bed, and hath fet himfelf in no good way : neither doth he abhor any thing that is evil.

5 Thy mercy, O Lord, reacheth unto the heavens : and thy faithfulnefs unto the clouds.

6 Thy righteoufnefs ftandeth like the ftrong mountains : thy judgements are like the great deep.

7 Thou, Lord, fhalt fave both man and beaft ; How excellent is thy mercy, O God : and the children of men fhall put their truft under the fhadow of thy wings.

8 They fhall be fatisfied with the plenteoufnefs of thy houfe : and thou fhalt give them drink of thy pleafures, as out of the river.

9 For with thee is the well of life : and in thy light fhall we fee light.

10 O continue forth thy loving-kindnefs unto them that know thee : and thy righteoufnefs unto them that are true of heart.

11 O let not the foot of pride come against me : and let not the hand of the ungodly caft me down.

12 There are they fallen, all that work wickednefs : they are caft down, and fhall not be able to ftand.

EVENING PRAYER

PSALM XXXVII.

NOLI ÆMULARI.

RET not thyfelf becaufe of the ungodly : neither be thou envious against the evil doers.

2 For they fhall foon be cut down like the grafs : and be withered even as the green herb.

3 Put thou thy truft in the

Lord, and be doing good : dwell in the land, and verily thou shalt be fed.

4 Delight thou in the Lord : and he shall give thee thy heart's desire.

5 Commit thy way unto the Lord, and put thy trust in him : and he shall bring it to pass.

6 He shall make thy righteousness as clear as the light : and thy just dealing as the noon-day.

7 Hold thee still in the Lord, and abide patiently upon him : but grieve not thyself at him, whose way doth prosper, against the man that doeth after evil counsels.

8 Leave off from wrath, and let go displeasure : fret not thyself, else shalt thou be moved to do evil.

9 Wicked doers shall be rooted out : and they that patiently abide the Lord, those shall inherit the land.

10 Yet a little while, and the ungodly shall be clean gone : thou shalt look after his place, and he shall be away.

11 But the meek-spirited shall possess the earth : and shall be refreshed in the multitude of peace.

12 The ungodly seeketh counsel against the just : and gnasheth upon him with his teeth.

13 The Lord shall laugh him to scorn : for he hath seen that his day is coming.

14 The ungodly have drawn out the sword, and have bent their bow : to cast down the poor and needy, and to slay such as are of a right conversation.

15 Their sword shall go through their own heart : and their bow shall be broken.

16 A small thing that the righteous hath : is better than great riches of the ungodly.

17 For the arms of the ungodly shall be broken : and the Lord upholdeth the righteous.

18 The Lord knoweth the days of the godly : and their inheritance shall endure for ever.

19 They shall not be confounded in the perilous time : and in the days of dearth they shall have enough.

20 As for the ungodly, they shall perish ; and the enemies of the Lord shall consume as the fat of lambs : yea, even as the smoke, shall they consume away.

21 The ungodly borroweth, and payeth not again : but the righteous is merciful, and liberal.

22 Such as are blessed of God shall possess the land : and they that are cursed of him shall be rooted out.

23 The Lord ordereth a good man's going : and maketh his way acceptable to himself.

24 Though he fall, he shall not be cast away : for the Lord upholdeth him with his hand.

25 I have been young, and now am old : and yet saw I never the righteous forsaken, nor his seed begging their bread.

26 The righteous is ever merciful, and lendeth : and his seed is blessed.

27 Flee from evil, and do the thing that is good : and dwell for evermore.

28 For the Lord loveth the thing that is right : he forsaketh not his that be godly, but they are preserved for ever.

29 The unrighteous shall be punished : as for the seed of the ungodly, it shall be rooted out.

30 The righteous shall inherit the land : and dwell therein for ever.

31 The mouth of the righteous is exercised in wisdom : and his tongue will be talking of judgement.

32 The law of his God is in his heart : and his goings shall not slide.

33 The ungodly seeth the righteous : and seeketh occasion to slay him.

34 The Lord will not leave him in his hand : nor condemn him when he is judged.

35 Hope thou in the Lord, and keep his way, and he shall promote thee, that thou shalt possess the land : when the ungodly shall perish, thou shalt see it.

36 I myself have seen the ungodly in great power : and flourishing like a green bay-tree.

37 I went by, and lo, he was gone : I sought him, but his place could no where be found.

38 Keep innocency, and take heed unto the thing that is right : for that shall bring a man peace at the last.

39 As for the transgressors, they shall perish together : and the end of the ungodly is, they shall be rooted out at the last.

40 But the salvation of the righteous cometh of the Lord : who is also their strength in the time of trouble.

41 And the Lord shall stand by them, and save them : he shall deliver them from the ungodly, and shall save them, because they put their trust in him.

MORNING PRAYER

PSALM XXXVIII.

DOMINE ME IN FURORE

Put me not to rebuke O Lord in thine anger neither chasten me in thy heavy displeasure

2 For thine arrows stick fast in me : and thy hand presseth me sore.

3 There is no health in my flesh, because of thy displeasure : neither is there any rest in my bones, by reason of my sin.

4 For my wickednesses are gone over my head : and are like a sore burden, too heavy for me to bear.

5 My wounds stink, and are corrupt : through my foolishness.

6 I am brought into so great trouble and misery : that I go mourning all the day long.

7 For my loins are filled with a sore disease : and there is no whole part in my body.

8 I am feeble, and sore smitten : I have roared for the very disquietness of my heart.

9 Lord, thou knowest all my desire : and my groaning is not hid from thee.

10 My heart panteth, my strength hath failed me : and the sight of mine eyes is gone from me.

11 My lovers and my neighbours did stand looking upon my trouble : and my kinsmen stood afar off.

12 They also that sought after my life laid snares for me : and they that went about to do me evil talked of wickedness, and imagined deceit all the day long.

13 As for me, I was like a deaf man, and heard not : and as one that is dumb, who doth not open his mouth.

14 I became even as a man that heareth not : and in whose mouth are no reproofs.

15 For in thee, O Lord, have I put my trust : thou shalt answer for me, O Lord my God.

16 I have required that they, even mine enemies, should not triumph over me : for when my foot slipped, they rejoiced greatly against me.

17 And I, truly, am set in the plague : and my heaviness is ever in my sight.

18 For I will confess my wickedness : and be sorry for my sin.

19 But mine enemies live, and are mighty : and they that hate me wrongfully are many in number.

20 They also that reward evil for good are against me : because I follow the thing that good is.

21 Forsake me not, O Lord my God : be not thou far from me.

22 Haste thee to help me : O Lord God of my salvation.

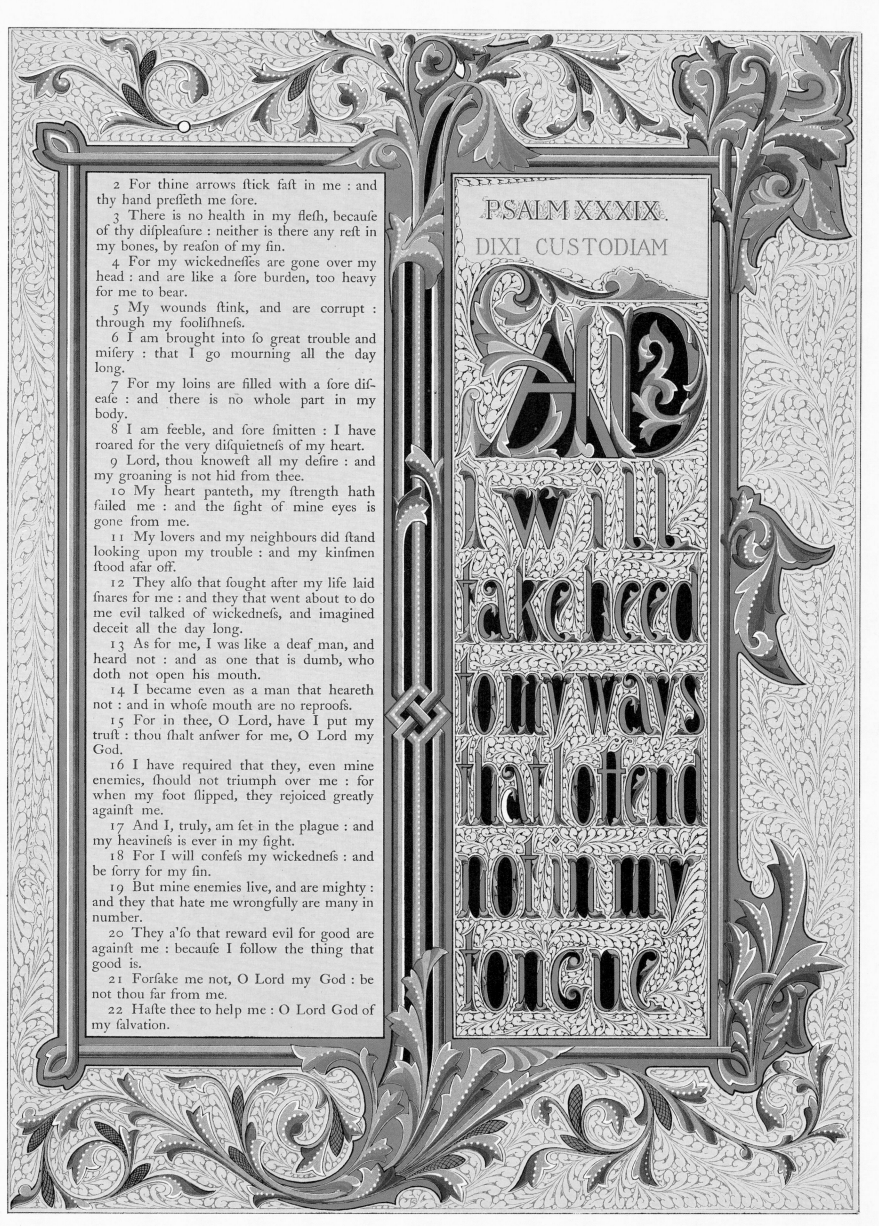

PSALM XXXIX.

DIXI CUSTODIAM

I SAID I will take heed to my ways that I offend not in my tongue

2 I will keep my mouth as it were with a bridle : while the ungodly is in my sight.

3 I held my tongue, and spake nothing : I kept silence, yea, even from good words; but it was pain and grief to me.

4 My heart was hot within me, and while I was thus musing the fire kindled : and at the last I spake with my tongue;

5 Lord, let me know mine end, and the number of my days : that I may be certified how long I have to live.

6 Behold, thou hast made my days as it were a span long : and mine age is even as nothing in respect of thee; and verily every man living is altogether vanity.

7 For man walketh in a vain shadow, and disquieteth himself in vain : he heapeth up riches, and cannot tell who shall gather them.

8 And now, Lord, what is my hope : truly my hope is even in thee.

9 Deliver me from all mine offences : and make me not a rebuke unto the foolish.

10 I became dumb, and opened not my mouth : for it was thy doing.

11 Take thy plague away from me : I am even consumed by the means of thy heavy hand.

12 When thou with rebukes dost chasten man for sin, thou makest his beauty to consume away, like as it were a moth fretting a garment : every man therefore is but vanity.

13 Hear my prayer, O Lord, and with thine ears consider my calling : hold not thy peace at my tears.

14 For I am a stranger with thee : and a sojourner, as all my fathers were.

15 O spare me a little, that I may recover my strength : before I go hence, and be no more seen.

Psalm XL.
Expectans expectavi.

I WAITED patiently for the Lord : and he inclined unto me, and heard my calling.

2 He brought me also out of the horrible pit, out of the mire and clay : and set my feet upon the rock, and ordered my goings.

3 And he hath put a new song in my mouth : even a thanksgiving unto our God.

4 Many shall see it, and fear : and shall put their trust in the Lord.

5 Blessed is the man that hath set his hope in the Lord : and turned not unto the proud, and to such as go about with lies.

6 O Lord my God, great are the wondrous works which thou hast done, like as be also thy thoughts which are to us-ward : and yet there is no man that ordereth them unto thee.

7 If I should declare them, and speak of them : they should be more than I am able to express.

8 Sacrifice, and meat-offering, thou wouldest not : but mine ears hast thou opened.

9 Burnt-offerings, and sacrifice for sin, hast thou not required : then said I, Lo, I come,

10 In the volume of the book it is written of me, that I should fulfil thy will, O my God : I am content to do it; yea, thy law is within my heart.

11 I have declared thy righteousness in the great congregation : lo, I will not refrain my lips, O Lord, and that thou knowest.

12 I have not hid thy righteousness within my heart : my talk hath been of thy truth, and of thy salvation.

13 I have not kept back thy loving mercy and truth : from the great congregation.

14 Withdraw not thou thy mercy from me, O Lord : let thy loving-kindness and thy truth alway preserve me.

15 For innumerable troubles are come about me; my sins have taken such hold upon me that I am not able to look up : yea, they are more in number than the hairs of my head, and my heart hath failed me.

16 O Lord, let it be thy pleasure to deliver me : make haste, O Lord, to help me.

17 Let them be ashamed, and confounded together, that seek after my soul to destroy it : let them be driven backward, and put to rebuke, that wish me evil.

18 Let them be desolate, and rewarded with shame : that say unto me, Fie upon thee, fie upon thee.

19 Let all those that seek thee be joyful and glad in thee : and let such as love thy salvation say alway, The Lord be praised.

20 As for me, I am poor and needy : but the Lord careth for me.

21 Thou art my helper and redeemer : make no long tarrying, O my God.

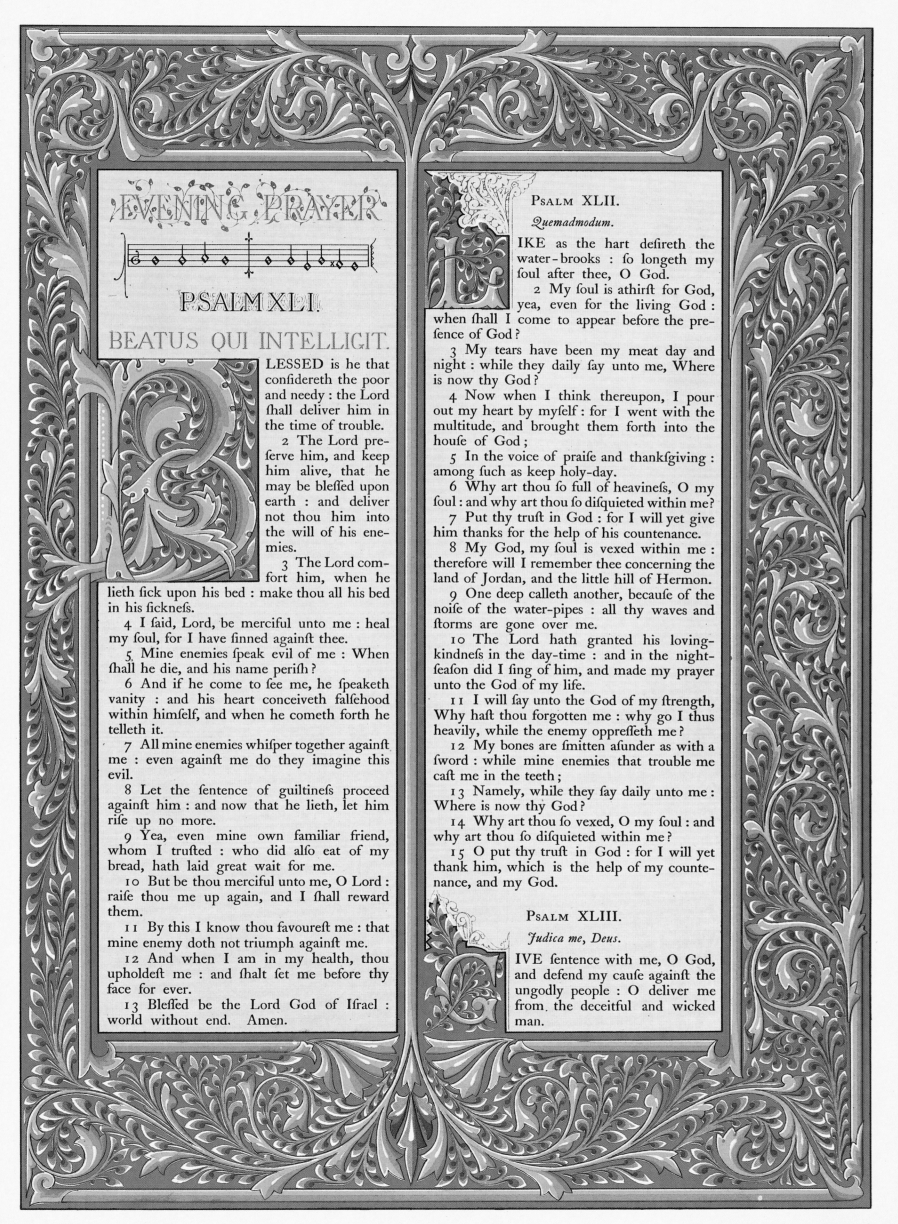

EVENING PRAYER

PSALM XLI.

BEATUS QUI INTELLIGIT.

LESSED is he that confidereth the poor and needy : the Lord fhall deliver him in the time of trouble.

2 The Lord preferve him, and keep him alive, that he may be bleffed upon earth : and deliver not thou him into the will of his enemies.

3 The Lord comfort him, when he lieth fick upon his bed : make thou all his bed in his ficknefs.

4 I faid, Lord, be merciful unto me : heal my foul, for I have finned againft thee.

5 Mine enemies fpeak evil of me : When fhall he die, and his name perifh ?

6 And if he come to fee me, he fpeaketh vanity : and his heart conceiveth falfehood within himfelf, and when he cometh forth he telleth it.

7 All mine enemies whifper together againft me : even againft me do they imagine this evil.

8 Let the fentence of guiltinefs proceed againft him : and now that he lieth, let him rife up no more.

9 Yea, even mine own familiar friend, whom I trufted : who did alfo eat of my bread, hath laid great wait for me.

10 But be thou merciful unto me, O Lord : raife thou me up again, and I fhall reward them.

11 By this I know thou favoureft me : that mine enemy doth not triumph againft me.

12 And when I am in my health, thou upholdeft me : and fhalt fet me before thy face for ever.

13 Bleffed be the Lord God of Ifrael : world without end. Amen.

PSALM XLII.

Quemadmodum.

IKE as the hart defireth the water-brooks : fo longeth my foul after thee, O God.

2 My foul is athirft for God, yea, even for the living God : when fhall I come to appear before the prefence of God ?

3 My tears have been my meat day and night : while they daily fay unto me, Where is now thy God ?

4 Now when I think thereupon, I pour out my heart by myfelf : for I went with the multitude, and brought them forth into the houfe of God ;

5 In the voice of praife and thankfgiving : among fuch as keep holy-day.

6 Why art thou fo full of heavinefs, O my foul : and why art thou fo difquieted within me ?

7 Put thy truft in God : for I will yet give him thanks for the help of his countenance.

8 My God, my foul is vexed within me : therefore will I remember thee concerning the land of Jordan, and the little hill of Hermon.

9 One deep calleth another, becaufe of the noife of the water-pipes : all thy waves and ftorms are gone over me.

10 The Lord hath granted his lovingkindnefs in the day-time : and in the nightfeafon did I fing of him, and made my prayer unto the God of my life.

11 I will fay unto the God of my ftrength, Why haft thou forgotten me : why go I thus heavily, while the enemy oppreffeth me ?

12 My bones are fmitten afunder as with a fword : while mine enemies that trouble me caft me in the teeth ;

13 Namely, while they fay daily unto me : Where is now thy God ?

14 Why art thou fo vexed, O my foul : and why art thou fo difquieted within me ?

15 O put thy truft in God : for I will yet thank him, which is the help of my countenance, and my God.

PSALM XLIII.

Judica me, Deus.

IVE fentence with me, O God, and defend my caufe againft the ungodly people : O deliver me from the deceitful and wicked man.

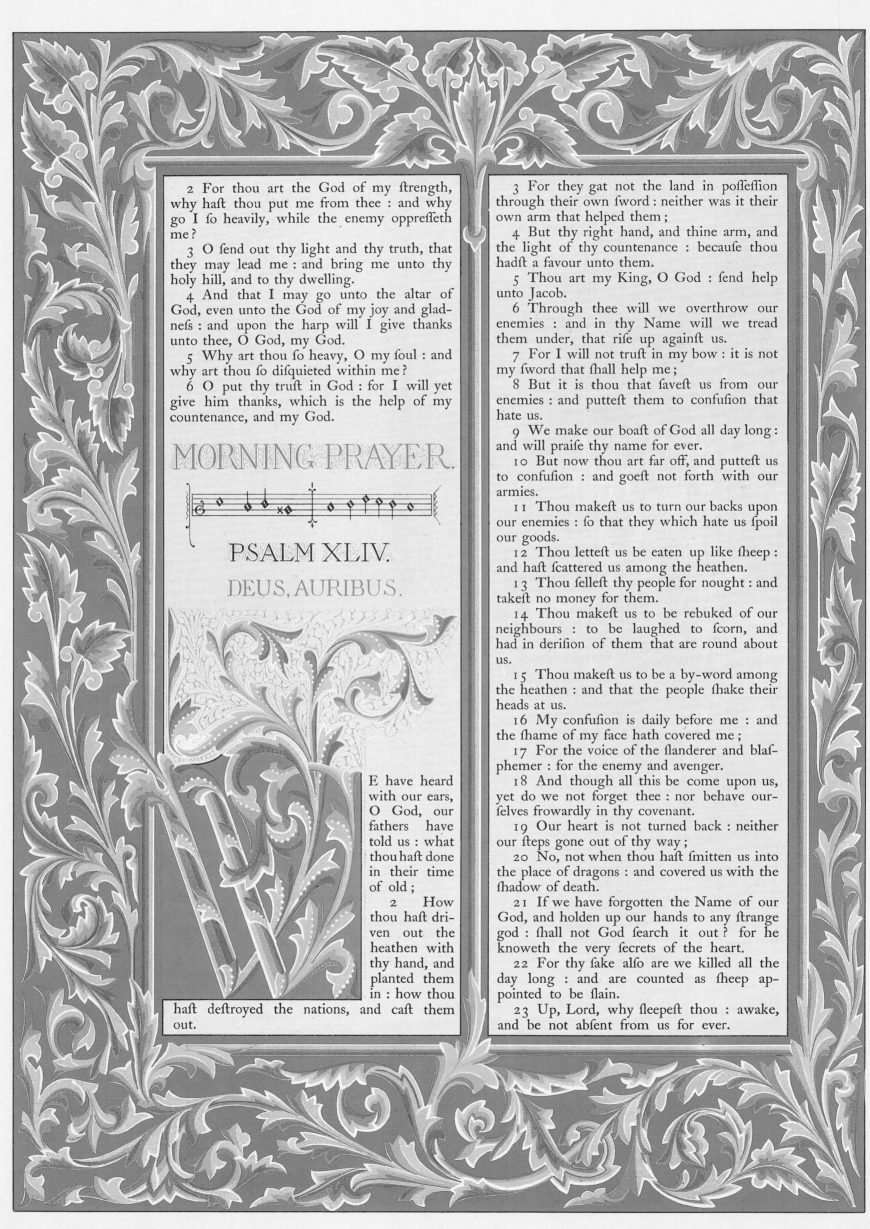

2 For thou art the God of my strength, why haft thou put me from thee : and why go I so heavily, while the enemy oppresseth me?

3 O send out thy light and thy truth, that they may lead me : and bring me unto thy holy hill, and to thy dwelling.

4 And that I may go unto the altar of God, even unto the God of my joy and gladness : and upon the harp will I give thanks unto thee, O God, my God.

5 Why art thou so heavy, O my soul : and why art thou so disquieted within me?

6 O put thy trust in God : for I will yet give him thanks, which is the help of my countenance, and my God.

MORNING PRAYER.

PSALM XLIV.

DEUS, AURIBUS.

W E have heard with our ears, O God, our fathers have told us : what thou haft done in their time of old ;

2 How thou haft driven out the heathen with thy hand, and planted them in : how thou haft destroyed the nations, and cast them out.

3 For they gat not the land in possession through their own sword : neither was it their own arm that helped them ;

4 But thy right hand, and thine arm, and the light of thy countenance : because thou hadst a favour unto them.

5 Thou art my King, O God : send help unto Jacob.

6 Through thee will we overthrow our enemies : and in thy Name will we tread them under, that rise up against us.

7 For I will not trust in my bow : it is not my sword that shall help me ;

8 But it is thou that savest us from our enemies : and puttest them to confusion that hate us.

9 We make our boast of God all day long : and will praise thy name for ever.

10 But now thou art far off, and puttest us to confusion : and goest not forth with our armies.

11 Thou makest us to turn our backs upon our enemies : so that they which hate us spoil our goods.

12 Thou lettest us be eaten up like sheep : and haft scattered us among the heathen.

13 Thou sellest thy people for nought : and takest no money for them.

14 Thou makest us to be rebuked of our neighbours : to be laughed to scorn, and had in derision of them that are round about us.

15 Thou makest us to be a by-word among the heathen : and that the people shake their heads at us.

16 My confusion is daily before me : and the shame of my face hath covered me ;

17 For the voice of the slanderer and blasphemer : for the enemy and avenger.

18 And though all this be come upon us, yet do we not forget thee : nor behave ourselves frowardly in thy covenant.

19 Our heart is not turned back : neither our steps gone out of thy way ;

20 No, not when thou haft smitten us into the place of dragons : and covered us with the shadow of death.

21 If we have forgotten the Name of our God, and holden up our hands to any strange god : shall not God search it out? for he knoweth the very secrets of the heart.

22 For thy sake also are we killed all the day long : and are counted as sheep appointed to be slain.

23 Up, Lord, why sleepest thou : awake, and be not absent from us for ever.

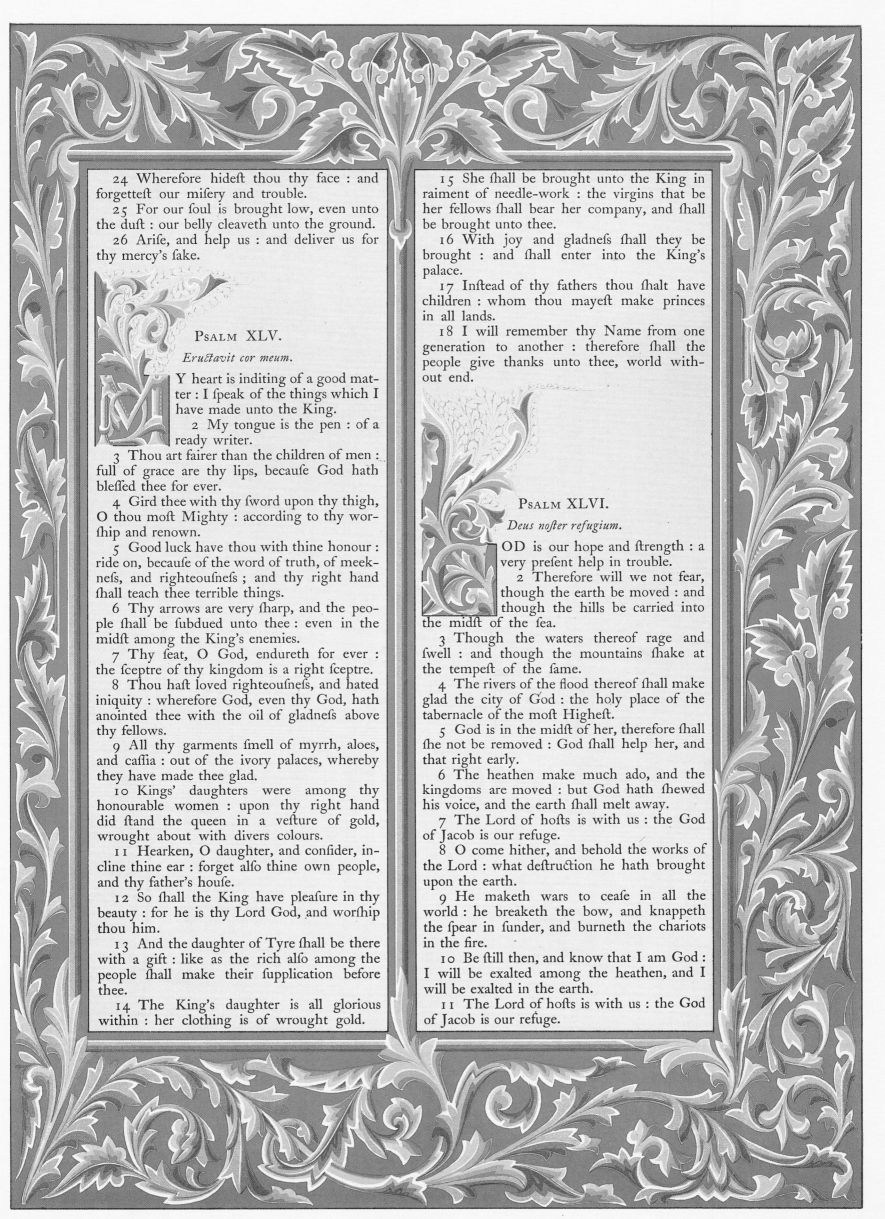

24 Wherefore hideſt thou thy face : and forgetteſt our miſery and trouble.

25 For our ſoul is brought low, even unto the duſt : our belly cleaveth unto the ground.

26 Ariſe, and help us : and deliver us for thy mercy's ſake.

Psalm XLV.
Eructavit cor meum.

MY heart is inditing of a good matter : I ſpeak of the things which I have made unto the King.

2 My tongue is the pen : of a ready writer.

3 Thou art fairer than the children of men : full of grace are thy lips, becauſe God hath bleſſed thee for ever.

4 Gird thee with thy ſword upon thy thigh, O thou moſt Mighty : according to thy worſhip and renown.

5 Good luck have thou with thine honour : ride on, becauſe of the word of truth, of meekneſs, and righteouſneſs ; and thy right hand ſhall teach thee terrible things.

6 Thy arrows are very ſharp, and the people ſhall be ſubdued unto thee : even in the midſt among the King's enemies.

7 Thy ſeat, O God, endureth for ever : the ſceptre of thy kingdom is a right ſceptre.

8 Thou haſt loved righteouſneſs, and hated iniquity : wherefore God, even thy God, hath anointed thee with the oil of gladneſs above thy fellows.

9 All thy garments ſmell of myrrh, aloes, and caſſia : out of the ivory palaces, whereby they have made thee glad.

10 Kings' daughters were among thy honourable women : upon thy right hand did ſtand the queen in a veſture of gold, wrought about with divers colours.

11 Hearken, O daughter, and conſider, incline thine ear : forget alſo thine own people, and thy father's houſe.

12 So ſhall the King have pleaſure in thy beauty : for he is thy Lord God, and worſhip thou him.

13 And the daughter of Tyre ſhall be there with a gift : like as the rich alſo among the people ſhall make their ſupplication before thee.

14 The King's daughter is all glorious within : her clothing is of wrought gold.

15 She ſhall be brought unto the King in raiment of needle-work : the virgins that be her fellows ſhall bear her company, and ſhall be brought unto thee.

16 With joy and gladneſs ſhall they be brought : and ſhall enter into the King's palace.

17 Inſtead of thy fathers thou ſhalt have children : whom thou mayeſt make princes in all lands.

18 I will remember thy Name from one generation to another : therefore ſhall the people give thanks unto thee, world without end.

Psalm XLVI.
Deus noster refugium.

GOD is our hope and ſtrength : a very preſent help in trouble.

2 Therefore will we not fear, though the earth be moved : and though the hills be carried into the midſt of the ſea.

3 Though the waters thereof rage and ſwell : and though the mountains ſhake at the tempeſt of the ſame.

4 The rivers of the flood thereof ſhall make glad the city of God : the holy place of the tabernacle of the moſt Higheſt.

5 God is in the midſt of her, therefore ſhall ſhe not be removed : God ſhall help her, and that right early.

6 The heathen make much ado, and the kingdoms are moved : but God hath ſhewed his voice, and the earth ſhall melt away.

7 The Lord of hoſts is with us : the God of Jacob is our refuge.

8 O come hither, and behold the works of the Lord : what deſtruction he hath brought upon the earth.

9 He maketh wars to ceaſe in all the world : he breaketh the bow, and knappeth the ſpear in ſunder, and burneth the chariots in the fire.

10 Be ſtill then, and know that I am God : I will be exalted among the heathen, and I will be exalted in the earth.

11 The Lord of hoſts is with us : the God of Jacob is our refuge.

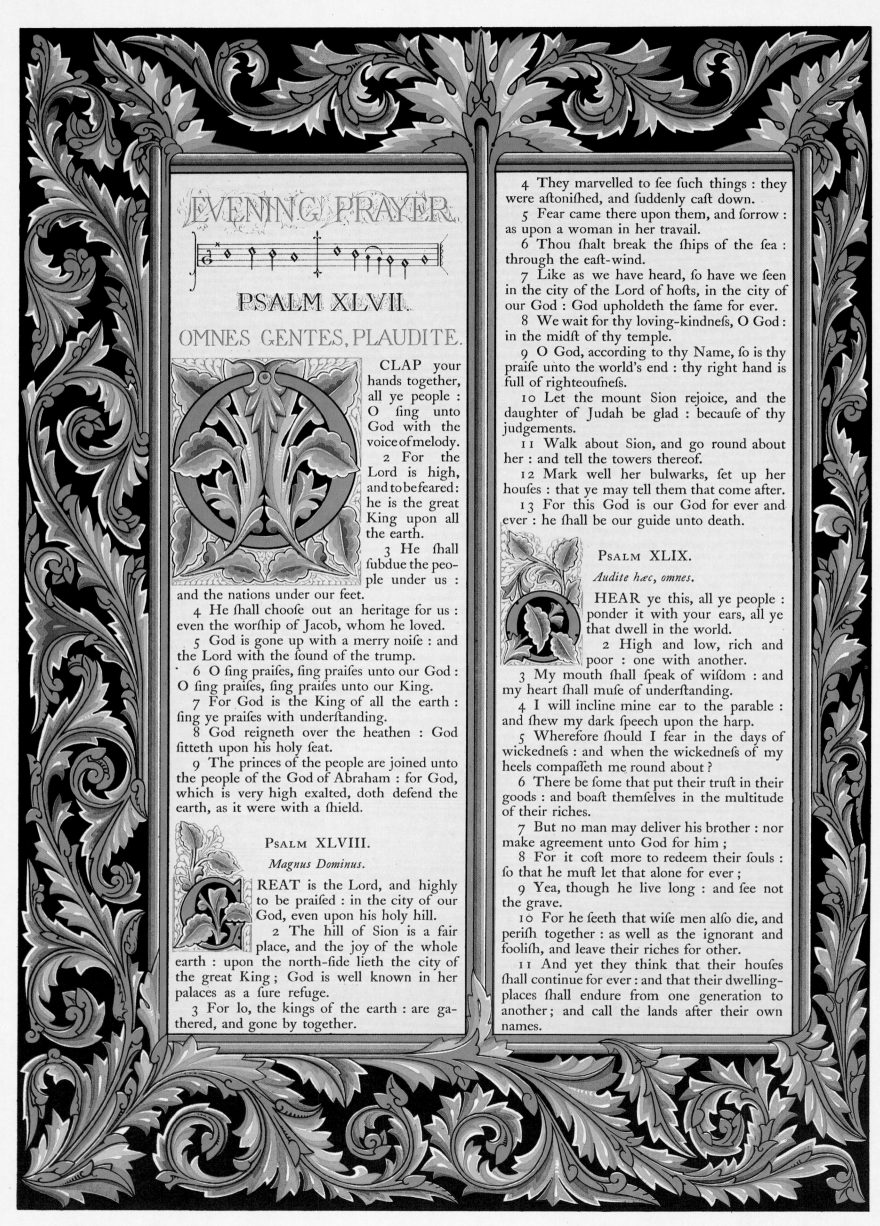

EVENING PRAYER.

PSALM XLVII.

OMNES GENTES, PLAUDITE.

CLAP your hands together, all ye people : O sing unto God with the voice of melody.

2 For the Lord is high, and to be feared : he is the great King upon all the earth.

3 He shall subdue the people under us : and the nations under our feet.

4 He shall choose out an heritage for us : even the worship of Jacob, whom he loved.

5 God is gone up with a merry noise : and the Lord with the sound of the trump.

6 O sing praises, sing praises unto our God : O sing praises, sing praises unto our King.

7 For God is the King of all the earth : sing ye praises with understanding.

8 God reigneth over the heathen : God sitteth upon his holy seat.

9 The princes of the people are joined unto the people of the God of Abraham : for God, which is very high exalted, doth defend the earth, as it were with a shield.

Psalm XLVIII.

Magnus Dominus.

GREAT is the Lord, and highly to be praised : in the city of our God, even upon his holy hill.

2 The hill of Sion is a fair place, and the joy of the whole earth : upon the north-side lieth the city of the great King ; God is well known in her palaces as a sure refuge.

3 For lo, the kings of the earth : are gathered, and gone by together.

4 They marvelled to see such things : they were astonished, and suddenly cast down.

5 Fear came there upon them, and sorrow : as upon a woman in her travail.

6 Thou shalt break the ships of the sea : through the east-wind.

7 Like as we have heard, so have we seen in the city of the Lord of hosts, in the city of our God : God upholdeth the same for ever.

8 We wait for thy loving-kindness, O God : in the midst of thy temple.

9 O God, according to thy Name, so is thy praise unto the world's end : thy right hand is full of righteousness.

10 Let the mount Sion rejoice, and the daughter of Judah be glad : because of thy judgements.

11 Walk about Sion, and go round about her : and tell the towers thereof.

12 Mark well her bulwarks, set up her houses : that ye may tell them that come after.

13 For this God is our God for ever and ever : he shall be our guide unto death.

Psalm XLIX.

Audite hæc, omnes.

HEAR ye this, all ye people : ponder it with your ears, all ye that dwell in the world.

2 High and low, rich and poor : one with another.

3 My mouth shall speak of wisdom : and my heart shall muse of understanding.

4 I will incline mine ear to the parable : and shew my dark speech upon the harp.

5 Wherefore should I fear in the days of wickedness : and when the wickedness of my heels compasseth me round about ?

6 There be some that put their trust in their goods : and boast themselves in the multitude of their riches.

7 But no man may deliver his brother : nor make agreement unto God for him ;

8 For it cost more to redeem their souls : so that he must let that alone for ever ;

9 Yea, though he live long : and see not the grave.

10 For he seeth that wise men also die, and perish together : as well as the ignorant and foolish, and leave their riches for other.

11 And yet they think that their houses shall continue for ever : and that their dwelling-places shall endure from one generation to another ; and call the lands after their own names.

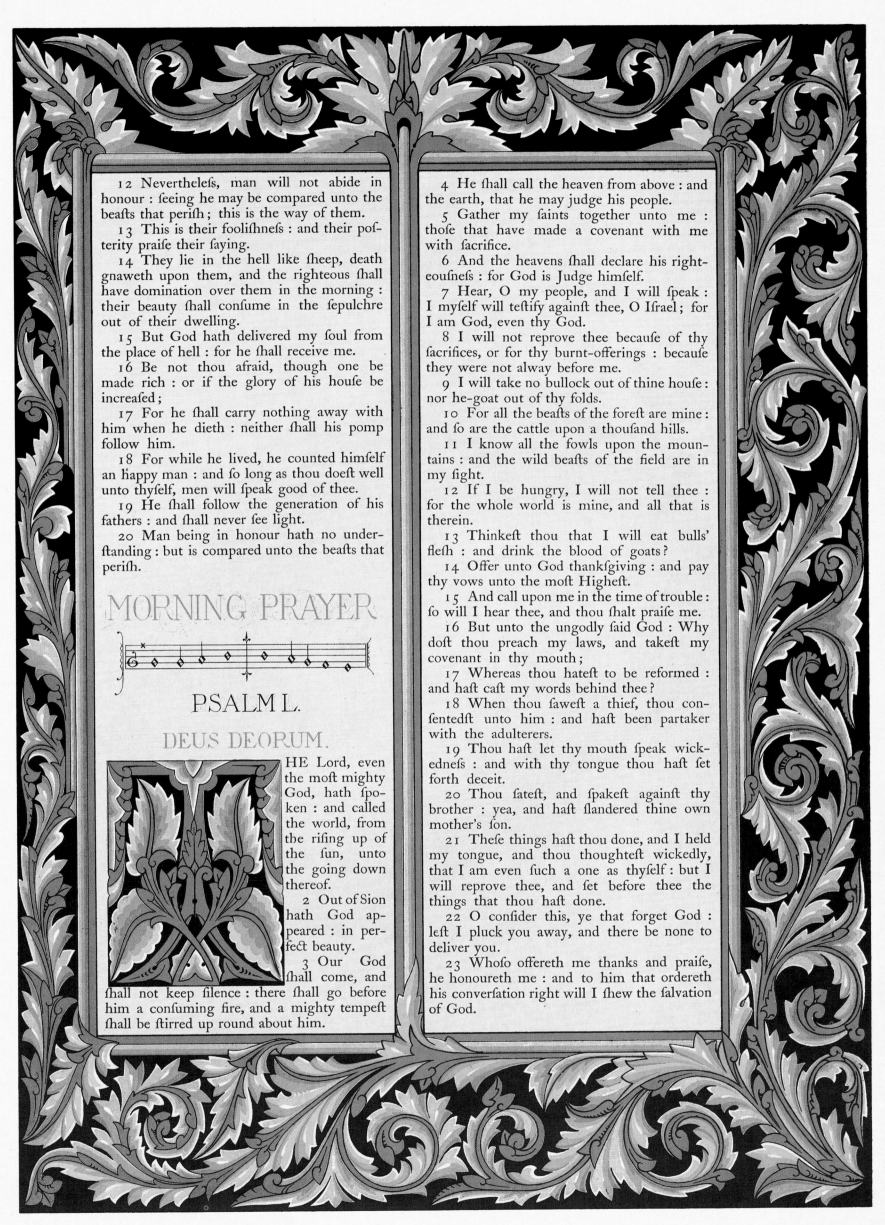

12 Neverthelefs, man will not abide in honour : feeing he may be compared unto the beafts that perifh ; this is the way of them.

13 This is their foolifhnefs : and their pofterity praife their faying.

14 They lie in the hell like fheep, death gnaweth upon them, and the righteous fhall have domination over them in the morning : their beauty fhall confume in the fepulchre out of their dwelling.

15 But God hath delivered my foul from the place of hell : for he fhall receive me.

16 Be not thou afraid, though one be made rich : or if the glory of his houfe be increafed ;

17 For he fhall carry nothing away with him when he dieth : neither fhall his pomp follow him.

18 For while he lived, he counted himfelf an happy man : and fo long as thou doeft well unto thyfelf, men will fpeak good of thee.

19 He fhall follow the generation of his fathers : and fhall never fee light.

20 Man being in honour hath no underftanding : but is compared unto the beafts that perifh.

MORNING PRAYER

PSALM L.

DEUS DEORUM.

HE Lord, even the moft mighty God, hath fpoken : and called the world, from the rifing up of the fun, unto the going down thereof.

2 Out of Sion hath God appeared : in perfect beauty.

3 Our God fhall come, and fhall not keep filence : there fhall go before him a confuming fire, and a mighty tempeft fhall be ftirred up round about him.

4 He fhall call the heaven from above : and the earth, that he may judge his people.

5 Gather my faints together unto me : thofe that have made a covenant with me with facrifice.

6 And the heavens fhall declare his righteoufnefs : for God is Judge himfelf.

7 Hear, O my people, and I will fpeak : I myfelf will teftify againft thee, O Ifrael ; for I am God, even thy God.

8 I will not reprove thee becaufe of thy facrifices, or for thy burnt-offerings : becaufe they were not alway before me.

9 I will take no bullock out of thine houfe : nor he-goat out of thy folds.

10 For all the beafts of the foreft are mine : and fo are the cattle upon a thoufand hills.

11 I know all the fowls upon the mountains : and the wild beafts of the field are in my fight.

12 If I be hungry, I will not tell thee : for the whole world is mine, and all that is therein.

13 Thinkeft thou that I will eat bulls' flefh : and drink the blood of goats ?

14 Offer unto God thankfgiving : and pay thy vows unto the moft Higheft.

15 And call upon me in the time of trouble : fo will I hear thee, and thou fhalt praife me.

16 But unto the ungodly faid God : Why doft thou preach my laws, and takeft my covenant in thy mouth ;

17 Whereas thou hateft to be reformed : and haft caft my words behind thee ?

18 When thou faweft a thief, thou confentedft unto him : and haft been partaker with the adulterers.

19 Thou haft let thy mouth fpeak wickednefs : and with thy tongue thou haft fet forth deceit.

20 Thou fateft, and fpakeft againft thy brother : yea, and haft flandered thine own mother's fon.

21 Thefe things haft thou done, and I held my tongue, and thou thoughteft wickedly, that I am even fuch a one as thyfelf : but I will reprove thee, and fet before thee the things that thou haft done.

22 O confider this, ye that forget God : left I pluck you away, and there be none to deliver you.

23 Whofo offereth me thanks and praife, he honoureth me : and to him that ordereth his converfation right will I fhew the falvation of God.

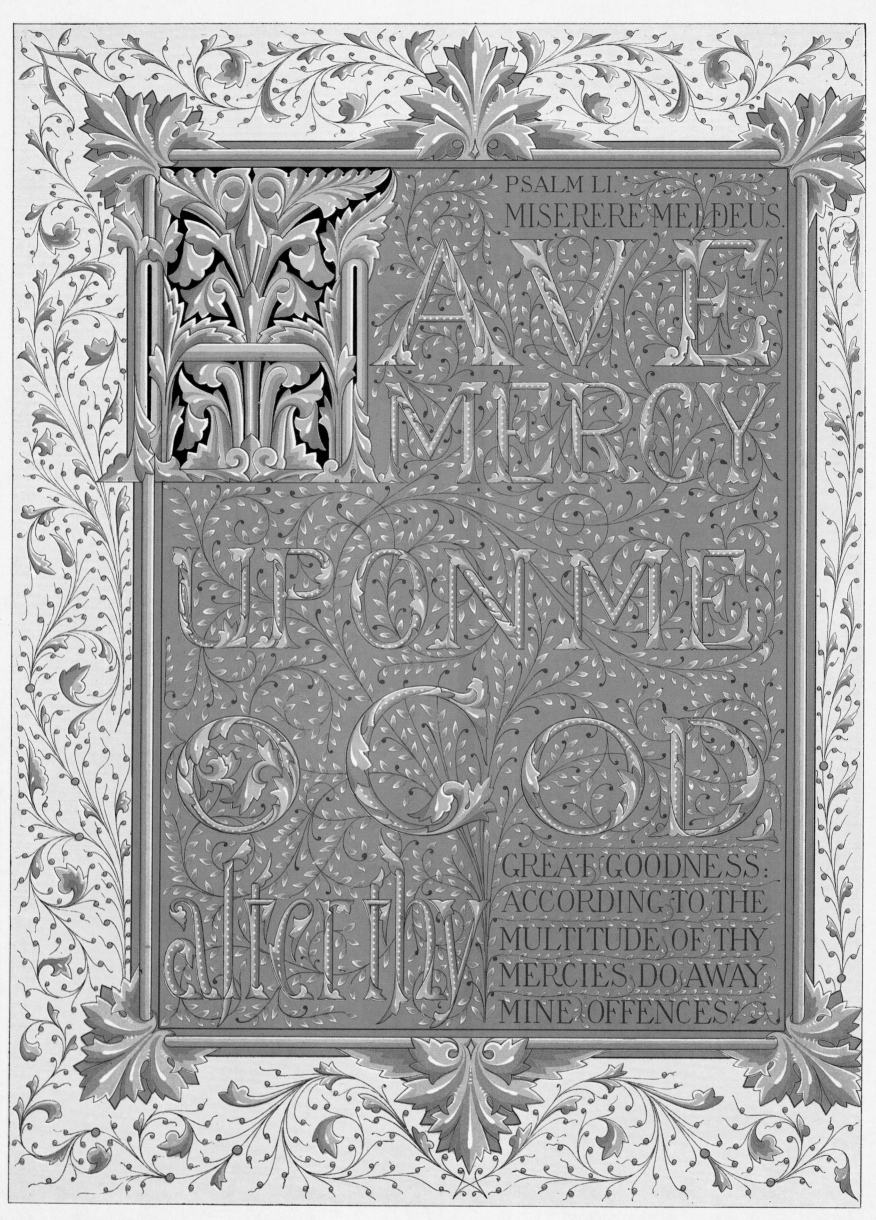

PSALM LI.
MISERERE MEI DEUS.

HAVE MERCY UPON ME O GOD

according to thy GREAT GOODNESS: ACCORDING TO THE MULTITUDE OF THY MERCIES DO AWAY MINE OFFENCES.

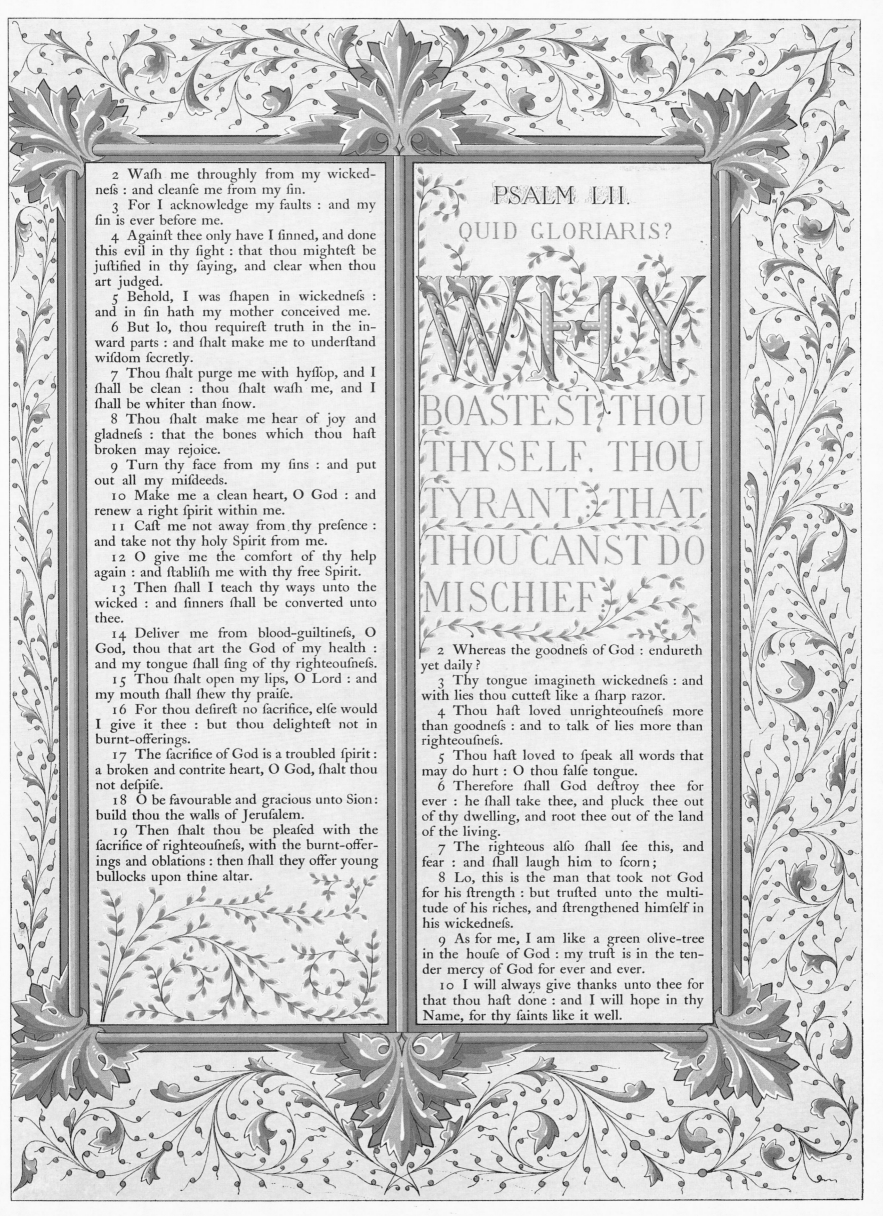

2 Wash me throughly from my wickedness : and cleanse me from my sin.

3 For I acknowledge my faults : and my sin is ever before me.

4 Against thee only have I sinned, and done this evil in thy sight : that thou mightest be justified in thy saying, and clear when thou art judged.

5 Behold, I was shapen in wickedness : and in sin hath my mother conceived me.

6 But lo, thou requirest truth in the inward parts : and shalt make me to understand wisdom secretly.

7 Thou shalt purge me with hyssop, and I shall be clean : thou shalt wash me, and I shall be whiter than snow.

8 Thou shalt make me hear of joy and gladness : that the bones which thou hast broken may rejoice.

9 Turn thy face from my sins : and put out all my misdeeds.

10 Make me a clean heart, O God : and renew a right spirit within me.

11 Cast me not away from thy presence : and take not thy holy Spirit from me.

12 O give me the comfort of thy help again : and stablish me with thy free Spirit.

13 Then shall I teach thy ways unto the wicked : and sinners shall be converted unto thee.

14 Deliver me from blood-guiltiness, O God, thou that art the God of my health : and my tongue shall sing of thy righteousness.

15 Thou shalt open my lips, O Lord : and my mouth shall shew thy praise.

16 For thou desirest no sacrifice, else would I give it thee : but thou delightest not in burnt-offerings.

17 The sacrifice of God is a troubled spirit : a broken and contrite heart, O God, shalt thou not despise.

18 O be favourable and gracious unto Sion : build thou the walls of Jerusalem.

19 Then shalt thou be pleased with the sacrifice of righteousness, with the burnt-offerings and oblations : then shall they offer young bullocks upon thine altar.

PSALM LII.

QUID GLORIARIS?

WHY

BOASTEST THOU THYSELF, THOU TYRANT : THAT THOU CANST DO MISCHIEF;

2 Whereas the goodness of God : endureth yet daily ?

3 Thy tongue imagineth wickedness : and with lies thou cuttest like a sharp razor.

4 Thou hast loved unrighteousness more than goodness : and to talk of lies more than righteousness.

5 Thou hast loved to speak all words that may do hurt : O thou false tongue.

6 Therefore shall God destroy thee for ever : he shall take thee, and pluck thee out of thy dwelling, and root thee out of the land of the living.

7 The righteous also shall see this, and fear : and shall laugh him to scorn;

8 Lo, this is the man that took not God for his strength : but trusted unto the multitude of his riches, and strengthened himself in his wickedness.

9 As for me, I am like a green olive-tree in the house of God : my trust is in the tender mercy of God for ever and ever.

10 I will always give thanks unto thee for that thou hast done : and I will hope in thy Name, for thy saints like it well.

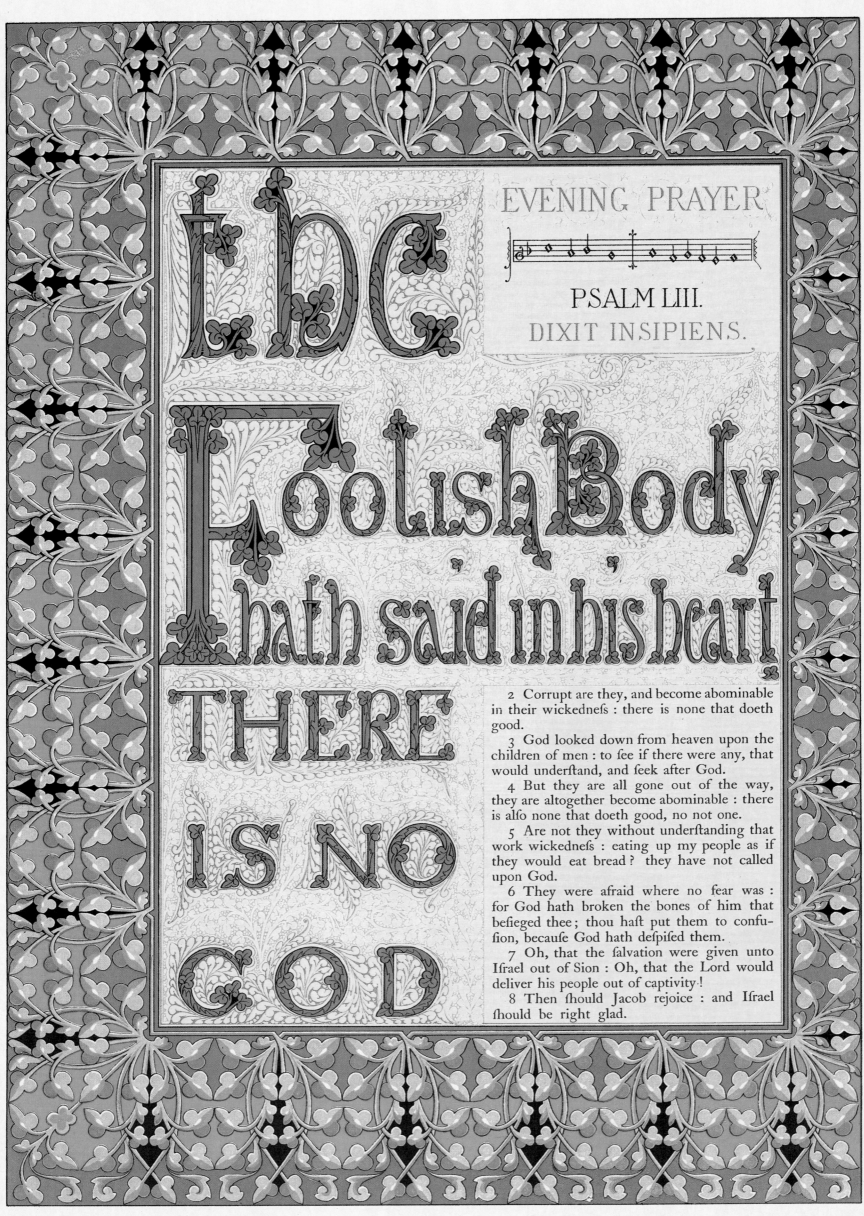

EVENING PRAYER

PSALM LIII.
DIXIT INSIPIENS.

The Foolish Body hath said in his heart THERE IS NO GOD

2 Corrupt are they, and become abominable in their wickedneſs : there is none that doeth good.

3 God looked down from heaven upon the children of men : to see if there were any, that would underſtand, and ſeek after God.

4 But they are all gone out of the way, they are altogether become abominable : there is alſo none that doeth good, no not one.

5 Are not they without underſtanding that work wickedneſs : eating up my people as if they would eat bread ? they have not called upon God.

6 They were afraid where no fear was : for God hath broken the bones of him that beſieged thee ; thou haſt put them to confuſion, becauſe God hath deſpiſed them.

7 Oh, that the ſalvation were given unto Iſrael out of Sion : Oh, that the Lord would deliver his people out of captivity !

8 Then ſhould Jacob rejoice : and Iſrael ſhould be right glad.

Psalm LIV.

Deus, in nomine.

SAVE me, O God, for thy Name's fake : and avenge me in thy ftrength.

2 Hear my prayer, O God : and hearken unto the words of my mouth.

3 For ftrangers are rifen up againft me : and tyrants, which have not God before their eyes, feek after my foul.

4 Behold, God is my helper : the Lord is with them that uphold my foul.

5 He fhall reward evil unto mine enemies : deftroy thou them in thy truth.

6 An offering of a free heart will I give thee, and praife thy Name, O Lord : becaufe it is fo comfortable.

7 For he hath delivered me out of all my trouble : and mine eye hath feen his defire upon mine enemies.

Psalm LV.

Exaudi, Deus.

HEAR my prayer, O God : and hide not thyfelf from my petition.

2 Take heed unto me, and hear me : how I mourn in my prayer, and am vexed.

3 The enemy crieth fo, and the ungodly cometh on fo faft : for they are minded to do me fome mifchief; fo malicioufly are they fet againft me.

4 My heart is difquieted within me : and the fear of death is fallen upon me.

5 Fearfulnefs and trembling are come upon me : and an horrible dread hath overwhelmed me.

6 And I faid, O that I had wings like a dove : for then would I flee away, and be at reft.

7 Lo, then would I get me away far off : and remain in the wildernefs.

8 I would make hafte to efcape : becaufe of the ftormy wind and tempeft.

9 Deftroy their tongues, O Lord, and divide them : for I have fpied unrighteoufnefs and ftrife in the city.

10 Day and night they go about within the walls thereof : mifchief alfo and forrow are in the midft of it.

11 Wickednefs is therein : deceit and guile go not out of their ftreets.

12 For it is not an open enemy, that hath done me this difhonour : for then I could have borne it.

13 Neither was it mine adverfary, that did magnify himfelf againft me : for then peradventure I would have hid myfelf from him.

14 But it was even thou, my companion : my guide, and mine own familiar friend.

15 We took fweet counfel together : and walked in the houfe of God as friends.

16 Let death come haftily upon them, and let them go down quick into hell : for wickednefs is in their dwellings, and among them.

17 As for me, I will call upon God : and the Lord fhall fave me.

18 In the evening, and morning, and at noon-day will I pray, and that inftantly : and he fhall hear my voice.

19 It is he that hath delivered my foul in peace from the battle that was againft me : for there were many with me.

20 Yea, even God, that endureth for ever, fhall hear me, and bring them down : for they will not turn, nor fear God.

21 He laid his hands upon fuch as be at peace with him : and he brake his covenant.

22 The words of his mouth were fofter than butter, having war in his heart : his words were fmoother than oil, and yet be they very fwords.

23 O caft thy burden upon the Lord, and he fhall nourifh thee : and fhall not fuffer the righteous to fall for ever.

24 And as for them : thou, O God, fhalt bring them into the pit of deftruction.

25 The blood-thirfty and deceitful men fhall not live out half their days : neverthelefs, my truft fhall be in thee, O Lord.

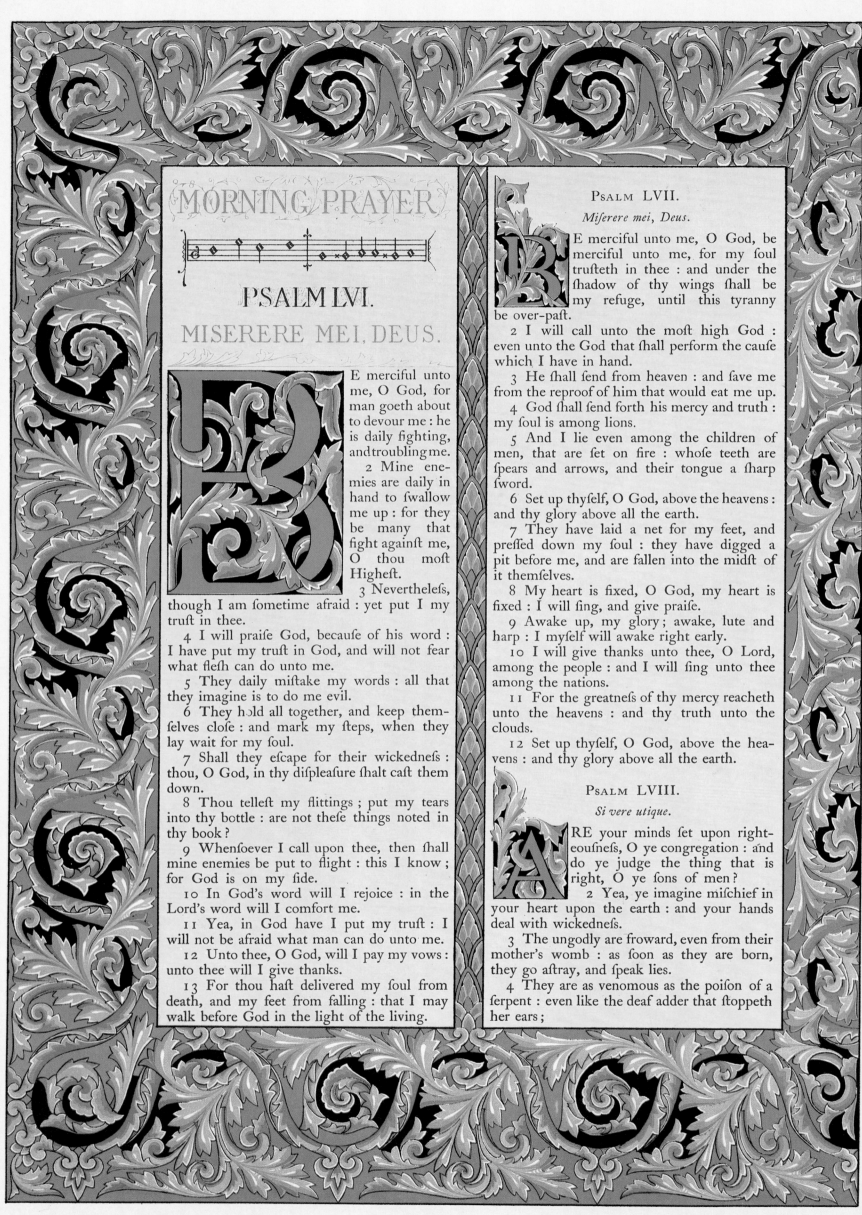

MORNING PRAYER

PSALM LVI.

MISERERE MEI, DEUS.

E merciful unto me, O God, for man goeth about to devour me : he is daily fighting, and troubling me.

2 Mine enemies are daily in hand to swallow me up : for they be many that fight against me, O thou most Highest.

3 Nevertheless, though I am sometime afraid : yet put I my trust in thee.

4 I will praise God, because of his word : I have put my trust in God, and will not fear what flesh can do unto me.

5 They daily mistake my words : all that they imagine is to do me evil.

6 They hold all together, and keep themselves close : and mark my steps, when they lay wait for my soul.

7 Shall they escape for their wickedness : thou, O God, in thy displeasure shalt cast them down.

8 Thou tellest my flittings ; put my tears into thy bottle : are not these things noted in thy book ?

9 Whensoever I call upon thee, then shall mine enemies be put to flight : this I know ; for God is on my side.

10 In God's word will I rejoice : in the Lord's word will I comfort me.

11 Yea, in God have I put my trust : I will not be afraid what man can do unto me.

12 Unto thee, O God, will I pay my vows : unto thee will I give thanks.

13 For thou hast delivered my soul from death, and my feet from falling : that I may walk before God in the light of the living.

PSALM LVII.

Miserere mei, Deus.

BE merciful unto me, O God, be merciful unto me, for my soul trusteth in thee : and under the shadow of thy wings shall be my refuge, until this tyranny be over-past.

2 I will call unto the most high God : even unto the God that shall perform the cause which I have in hand.

3 He shall send from heaven : and save me from the reproof of him that would eat me up.

4 God shall send forth his mercy and truth : my soul is among lions.

5 And I lie even among the children of men, that are set on fire : whose teeth are spears and arrows, and their tongue a sharp sword.

6 Set up thyself, O God, above the heavens : and thy glory above all the earth.

7 They have laid a net for my feet, and pressed down my soul : they have digged a pit before me, and are fallen into the midst of it themselves.

8 My heart is fixed, O God, my heart is fixed : I will sing, and give praise.

9 Awake up, my glory ; awake, lute and harp : I myself will awake right early.

10 I will give thanks unto thee, O Lord, among the people : and I will sing unto thee among the nations.

11 For the greatness of thy mercy reacheth unto the heavens : and thy truth unto the clouds.

12 Set up thyself, O God, above the heavens : and thy glory above all the earth.

PSALM LVIII.

Si vere utique.

ARE your minds set upon righteousness, O ye congregation : and do ye judge the thing that is right, O ye sons of men ?

2 Yea, ye imagine mischief in your heart upon the earth : and your hands deal with wickedness.

3 The ungodly are froward, even from their mother's womb : as soon as they are born, they go astray, and speak lies.

4 They are as venomous as the poison of a serpent : even like the deaf adder that stoppeth her ears ;

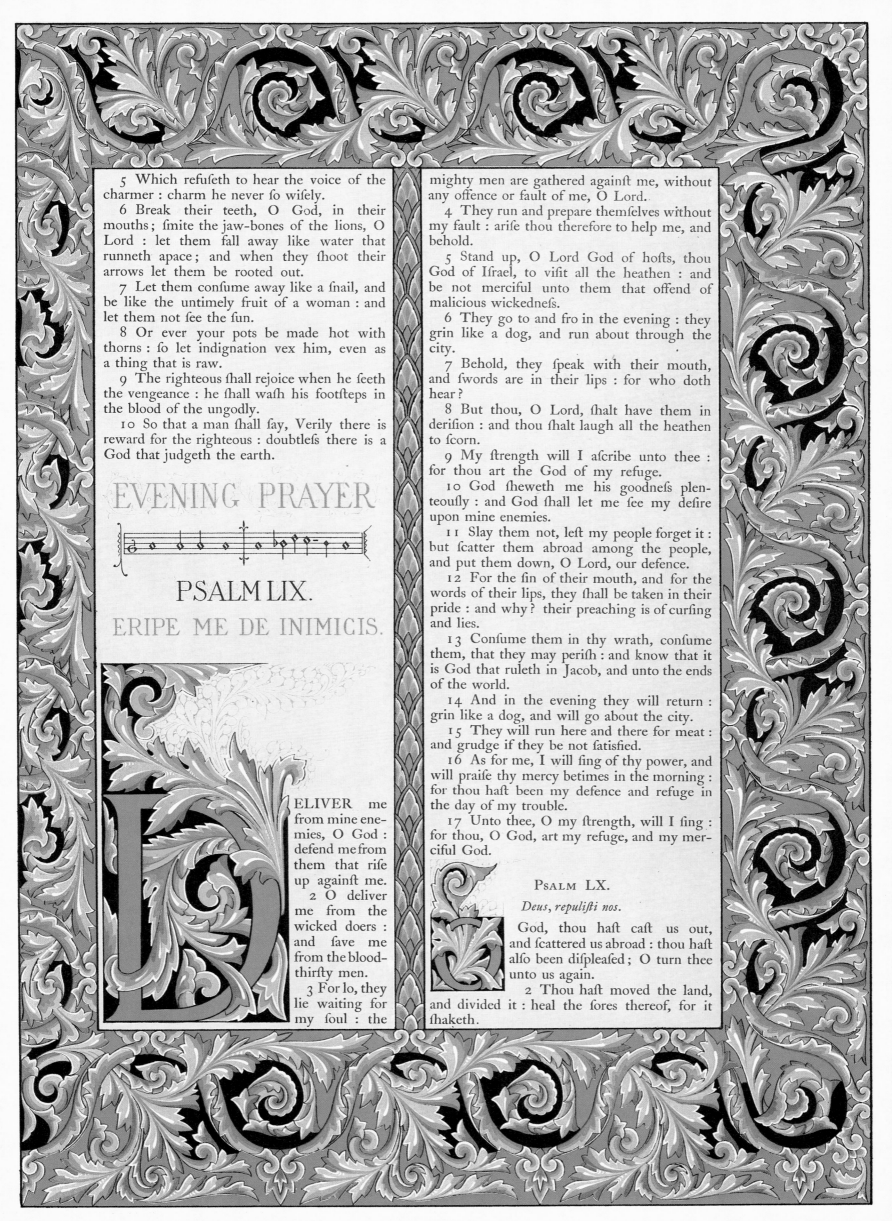

5 Which refuſeth to hear the voice of the charmer : charm he never ſo wiſely.

6 Break their teeth, O God, in their mouths; ſmite the jaw-bones of the lions, O Lord : let them fall away like water that runneth apace; and when they ſhoot their arrows let them be rooted out.

7 Let them conſume away like a ſnail, and be like the untimely fruit of a woman : and let them not ſee the ſun.

8 Or ever your pots be made hot with thorns : ſo let indignation vex him, even as a thing that is raw.

9 The righteous ſhall rejoice when he ſeeth the vengeance : he ſhall waſh his footſteps in the blood of the ungodly.

10 So that a man ſhall ſay, Verily there is reward for the righteous : doubtleſs there is a God that judgeth the earth.

EVENING PRAYER

PSALM LIX.

ERIPE ME DE INIMICIS.

ELIVER me from mine ene-mies, O God : defend me from them that riſe up againſt me.

2 O deliver me from the wicked doers : and ſave me from the blood-thirſty men.

3 For lo, they lie waiting for my ſoul : the mighty men are gathered againſt me, without any offence or fault of me, O Lord.

4 They run and prepare themſelves without my fault : ariſe thou therefore to help me, and behold.

5 Stand up, O Lord God of hoſts, thou God of Iſrael, to viſit all the heathen : and be not merciful unto them that offend of malicious wickedneſs.

6 They go to and fro in the evening : they grin like a dog, and run about through the city.

7 Behold, they ſpeak with their mouth, and ſwords are in their lips : for who doth hear?

8 But thou, O Lord, ſhalt have them in deriſion : and thou ſhalt laugh all the heathen to ſcorn.

9 My ſtrength will I aſcribe unto thee : for thou art the God of my refuge.

10 God ſheweth me his goodneſs plen-teouſly : and God ſhall let me ſee my deſire upon mine enemies.

11 Slay them not, leſt my people forget it : but ſcatter them abroad among the people, and put them down, O Lord, our defence.

12 For the ſin of their mouth, and for the words of their lips, they ſhall be taken in their pride : and why? their preaching is of curſing and lies.

13 Conſume them in thy wrath, conſume them, that they may periſh : and know that it is God that ruleth in Jacob, and unto the ends of the world.

14 And in the evening they will return : grin like a dog, and will go about the city.

15 They will run here and there for meat : and grudge if they be not ſatisfied.

16 As for me, I will ſing of thy power, and will praiſe thy mercy betimes in the morning : for thou haſt been my defence and refuge in the day of my trouble.

17 Unto thee, O my ſtrength, will I ſing : for thou, O God, art my refuge, and my mer-ciful God.

PSALM LX.

Deus, repuliſti nos.

God, thou haſt caſt us out, and ſcattered us abroad : thou haſt alſo been diſpleaſed; O turn thee unto us again.

2 Thou haſt moved the land, and divided it : heal the ſores thereof, for it ſhaketh.

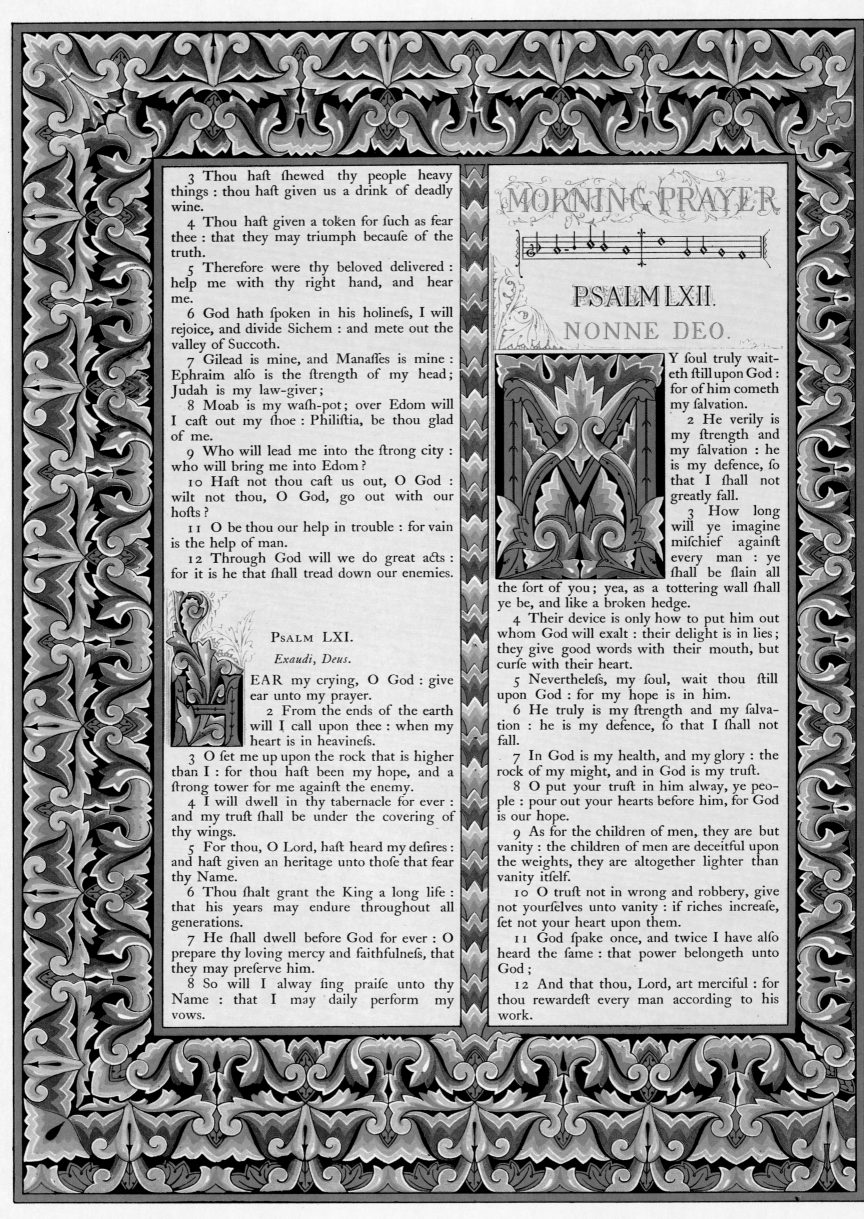

3 Thou haſt ſhewed thy people heavy things : thou haſt given us a drink of deadly wine.

4 Thou haſt given a token for ſuch as fear thee : that they may triumph becauſe of the truth.

5 Therefore were thy beloved delivered : help me with thy right hand, and hear me.

6 God hath ſpoken in his holineſs, I will rejoice, and divide Sichem : and mete out the valley of Succoth.

7 Gilead is mine, and Manaſſes is mine : Ephraim alſo is the ſtrength of my head; Judah is my law-giver;

8 Moab is my waſh-pot; over Edom will I caſt out my ſhoe : Philiſtia, be thou glad of me.

9 Who will lead me into the ſtrong city : who will bring me into Edom?

10 Haſt not thou caſt us out, O God : wilt not thou, O God, go out with our hoſts?

11 O be thou our help in trouble : for vain is the help of man.

12 Through God will we do great acts : for it is he that ſhall tread down our enemies.

Psalm LXI.
Exaudi, Deus.

EAR my crying, O God : give ear unto my prayer.

2 From the ends of the earth will I call upon thee : when my heart is in heavineſs.

3 O ſet me up upon the rock that is higher than I : for thou haſt been my hope, and a ſtrong tower for me againſt the enemy.

4 I will dwell in thy tabernacle for ever : and my truſt ſhall be under the covering of thy wings.

5 For thou, O Lord, haſt heard my deſires : and haſt given an heritage unto thoſe that fear thy Name.

6 Thou ſhalt grant the King a long life : that his years may endure throughout all generations.

7 He ſhall dwell before God for ever : O prepare thy loving mercy and faithfulneſs, that they may preſerve him.

8 So will I alway ſing praiſe unto thy Name : that I may daily perform my vows.

MORNING PRAYER

PSALM LXII.
NONNE DEO.

Y ſoul truly waiteth ſtill upon God : for of him cometh my ſalvation.

2 He verily is my ſtrength and my ſalvation : he is my defence, ſo that I ſhall not greatly fall.

3 How long will ye imagine miſchief againſt every man : ye ſhall be ſlain all the ſort of you; yea, as a tottering wall ſhall ye be, and like a broken hedge.

4 Their device is only how to put him out whom God will exalt : their delight is in lies; they give good words with their mouth, but curſe with their heart.

5 Nevertheleſs, my ſoul, wait thou ſtill upon God : for my hope is in him.

6 He truly is my ſtrength and my ſalvation : he is my defence, ſo that I ſhall not fall.

7 In God is my health, and my glory : the rock of my might, and in God is my truſt.

8 O put your truſt in him alway, ye people : pour out your hearts before him, for God is our hope.

9 As for the children of men, they are but vanity : the children of men are deceitful upon the weights, they are altogether lighter than vanity itſelf.

10 O truſt not in wrong and robbery, give not yourſelves unto vanity : if riches increaſe, ſet not your heart upon them.

11 God ſpake once, and twice I have alſo heard the ſame : that power belongeth unto God;

12 And that thou, Lord, art merciful : for thou rewardeſt every man according to his work.

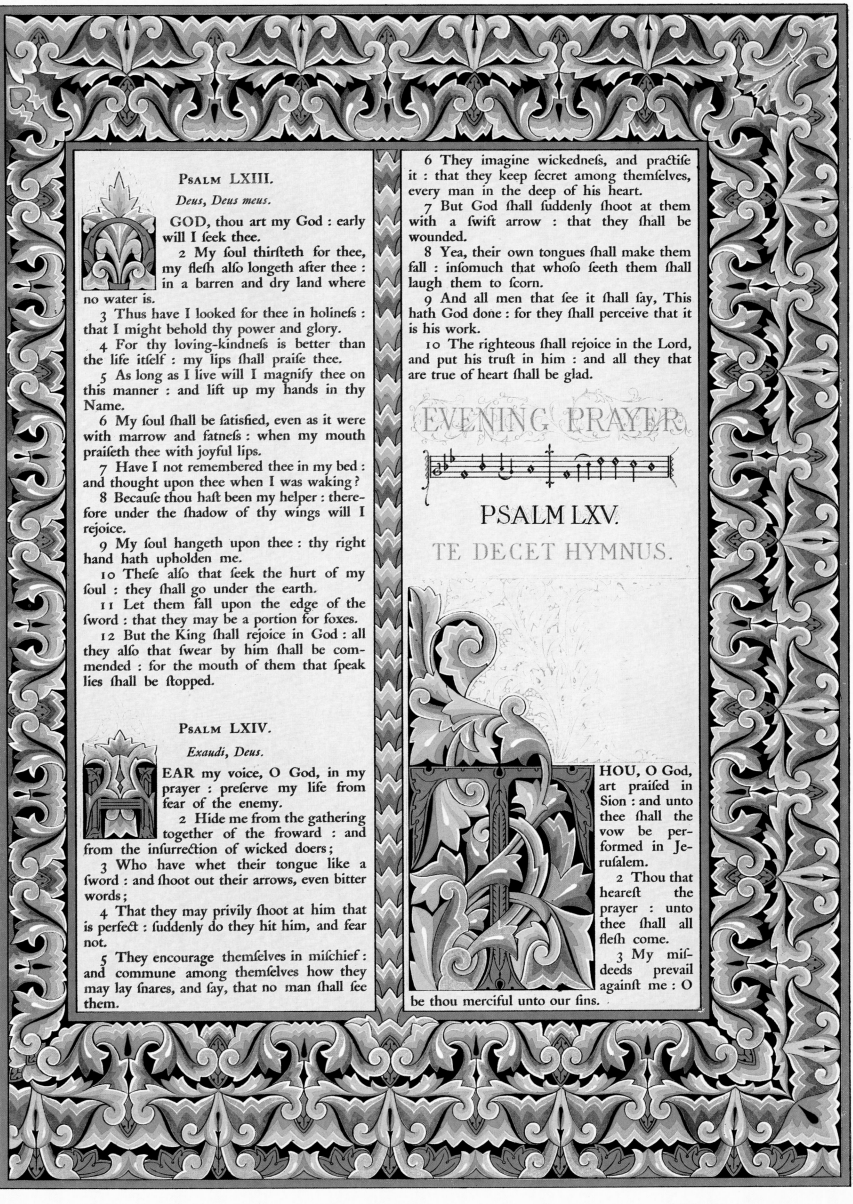

PSALM LXIII.

Deus, Deus meus.

GOD, thou art my God : early will I seek thee.

2 My soul thirsteth for thee, my flesh also longeth after thee : in a barren and dry land where no water is.

3 Thus have I looked for thee in holiness : that I might behold thy power and glory.

4 For thy loving-kindness is better than the life itself : my lips shall praise thee.

5 As long as I live will I magnify thee on this manner : and lift up my hands in thy Name.

6 My soul shall be satisfied, even as it were with marrow and fatness : when my mouth praiseth thee with joyful lips.

7 Have I not remembered thee in my bed : and thought upon thee when I was waking?

8 Because thou hast been my helper : therefore under the shadow of thy wings will I rejoice.

9 My soul hangeth upon thee : thy right hand hath upholden me.

10 These also that seek the hurt of my soul : they shall go under the earth.

11 Let them fall upon the edge of the sword : that they may be a portion for foxes.

12 But the King shall rejoice in God : all they also that swear by him shall be commended : for the mouth of them that speak lies shall be stopped.

PSALM LXIV.

Exaudi, Deus.

EAR my voice, O God, in my prayer : preserve my life from fear of the enemy.

2 Hide me from the gathering together of the froward : and from the insurrection of wicked doers;

3 Who have whet their tongue like a sword : and shoot out their arrows, even bitter words;

4 That they may privily shoot at him that is perfect : suddenly do they hit him, and fear not.

5 They encourage themselves in mischief : and commune among themselves how they may lay snares, and say, that no man shall see them.

6 They imagine wickedness, and practise it : that they keep secret among themselves, every man in the deep of his heart.

7 But God shall suddenly shoot at them with a swift arrow : that they shall be wounded.

8 Yea, their own tongues shall make them fall : insomuch that whoso seeth them shall laugh them to scorn.

9 And all men that see it shall say, This hath God done : for they shall perceive that it is his work.

10 The righteous shall rejoice in the Lord, and put his trust in him : and all they that are true of heart shall be glad.

EVENING PRAYER

PSALM LXV.

TE DECET HYMNUS.

THOU, O God, art praised in Sion : and unto thee shall the vow be performed in Jerusalem.

2 Thou that hearest the prayer : unto thee shall all flesh come.

3 My misdeeds prevail against me : O be thou merciful unto our sins.

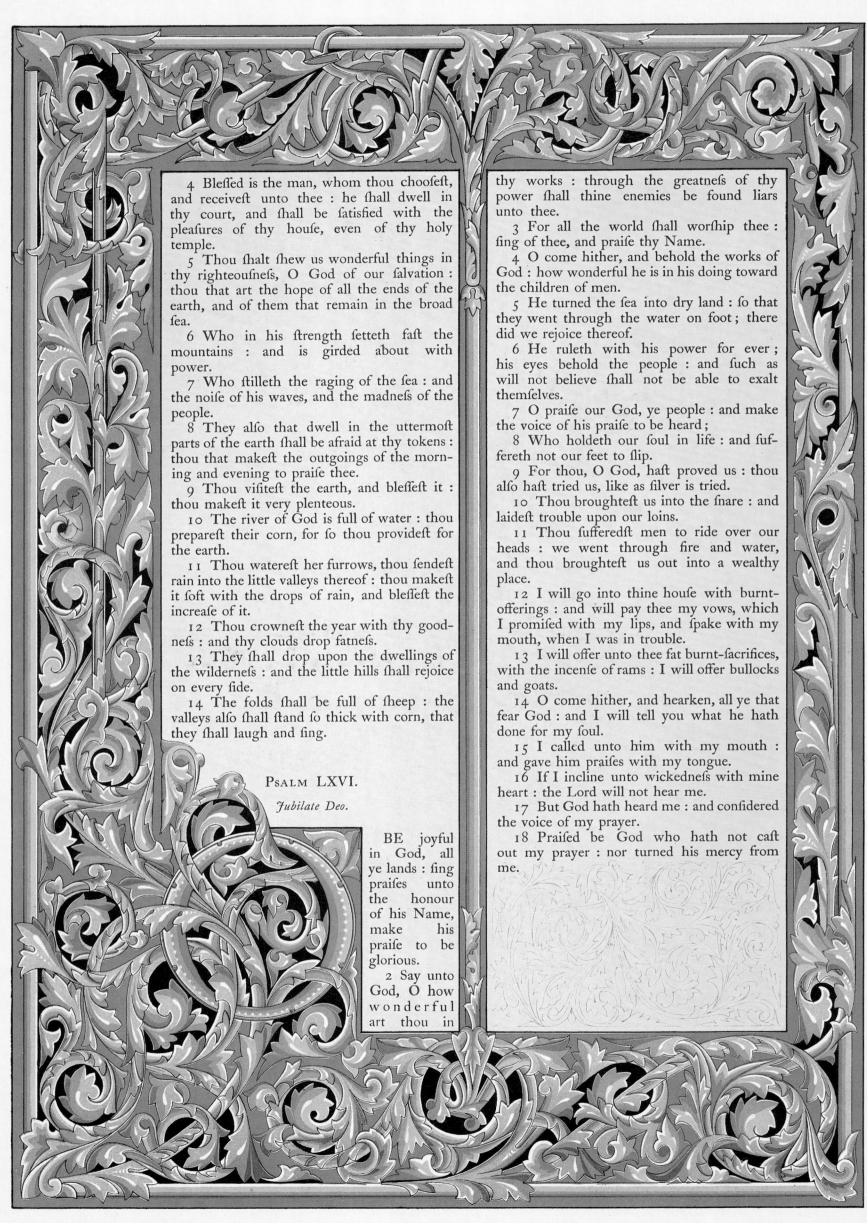

4 Blessed is the man, whom thou choosest, and receivest unto thee : he shall dwell in thy court, and shall be satisfied with the pleasures of thy house, even of thy holy temple.

5 Thou shalt shew us wonderful things in thy righteousness, O God of our salvation : thou that art the hope of all the ends of the earth, and of them that remain in the broad sea.

6 Who in his strength setteth fast the mountains : and is girded about with power.

7 Who stilleth the raging of the sea : and the noise of his waves, and the madness of the people.

8 They also that dwell in the uttermost parts of the earth shall be afraid at thy tokens : thou that makest the outgoings of the morning and evening to praise thee.

9 Thou visitest the earth, and blessest it : thou makest it very plenteous.

10 The river of God is full of water : thou preparest their corn, for so thou providest for the earth.

11 Thou waterest her furrows, thou sendest rain into the little valleys thereof : thou makest it soft with the drops of rain, and blessest the increase of it.

12 Thou crownest the year with thy goodness : and thy clouds drop fatness.

13 They shall drop upon the dwellings of the wilderness : and the little hills shall rejoice on every side.

14 The folds shall be full of sheep : the valleys also shall stand so thick with corn, that they shall laugh and sing.

Psalm LXVI.

Jubilate Deo.

BE joyful in God, all ye lands : sing praises unto the honour of his Name, make his praise to be glorious.

2 Say unto God, O how wonderful art thou in thy works : through the greatness of thy power shall thine enemies be found liars unto thee.

3 For all the world shall worship thee : sing of thee, and praise thy Name.

4 O come hither, and behold the works of God : how wonderful he is in his doing toward the children of men.

5 He turned the sea into dry land : so that they went through the water on foot; there did we rejoice thereof.

6 He ruleth with his power for ever; his eyes behold the people : and such as will not believe shall not be able to exalt themselves.

7 O praise our God, ye people : and make the voice of his praise to be heard;

8 Who holdeth our soul in life : and suffereth not our feet to slip.

9 For thou, O God, hast proved us : thou also hast tried us, like as silver is tried.

10 Thou broughtest us into the snare : and laidest trouble upon our loins.

11 Thou sufferedst men to ride over our heads : we went through fire and water, and thou broughtest us out into a wealthy place.

12 I will go into thine house with burnt-offerings : and will pay thee my vows, which I promised with my lips, and spake with my mouth, when I was in trouble.

13 I will offer unto thee fat burnt-sacrifices, with the incense of rams : I will offer bullocks and goats.

14 O come hither, and hearken, all ye that fear God : and I will tell you what he hath done for my soul.

15 I called unto him with my mouth : and gave him praises with my tongue.

16 If I incline unto wickedness with mine heart : the Lord will not hear me.

17 But God hath heard me : and considered the voice of my prayer.

18 Praised be God who hath not cast out my prayer : nor turned his mercy from me.

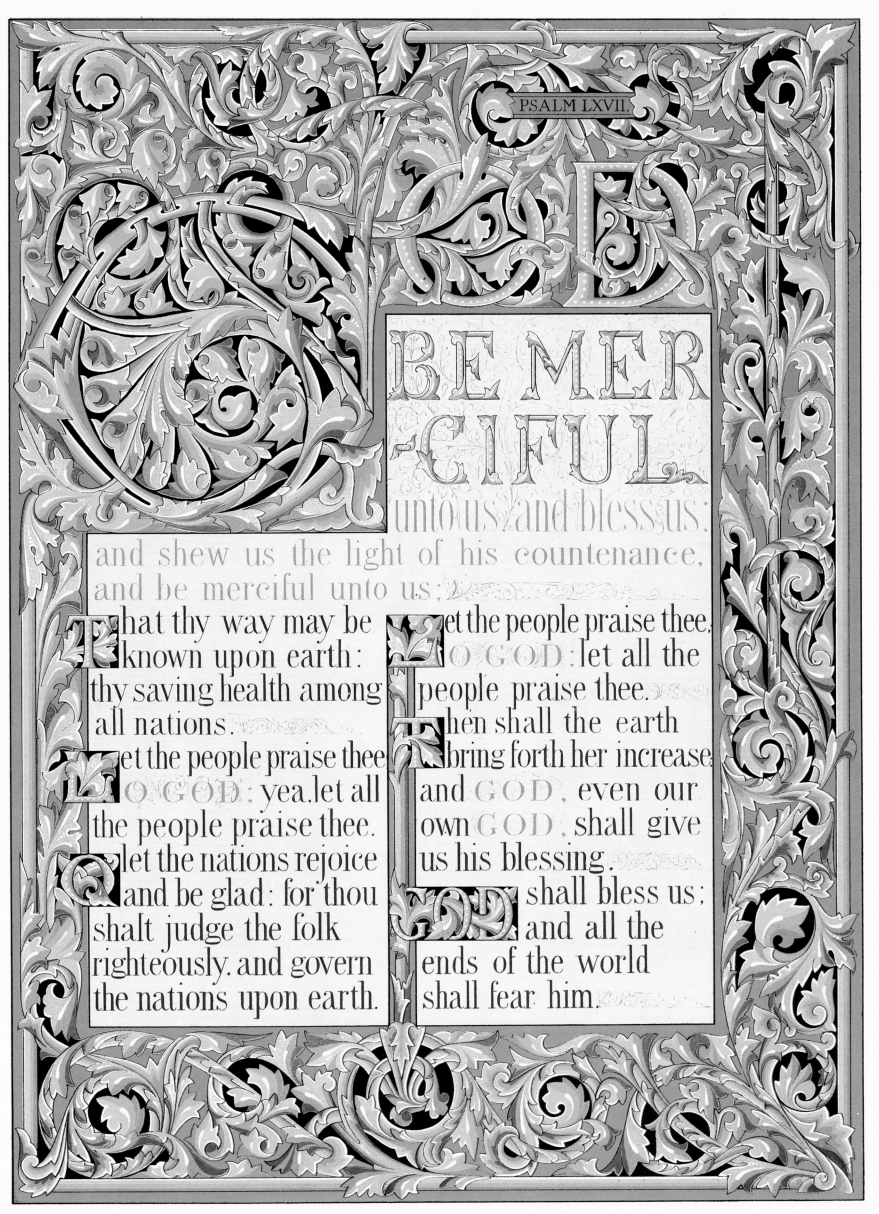

GOD BE MERCIFUL unto us, and bless us; and shew us the light of his countenance, and be merciful unto us;

That thy way may be known upon earth: thy saving health among all nations.

Let the people praise thee O GOD: yea, let all the people praise thee.

O let the nations rejoice and be glad: for thou shalt judge the folk righteously, and govern the nations upon earth.

Let the people praise thee, O GOD: let all the people praise thee.

Then shall the earth bring forth her increase; and GOD, even our own GOD, shall give us his blessing.

GOD shall bless us; and all the ends of the world shall fear him.

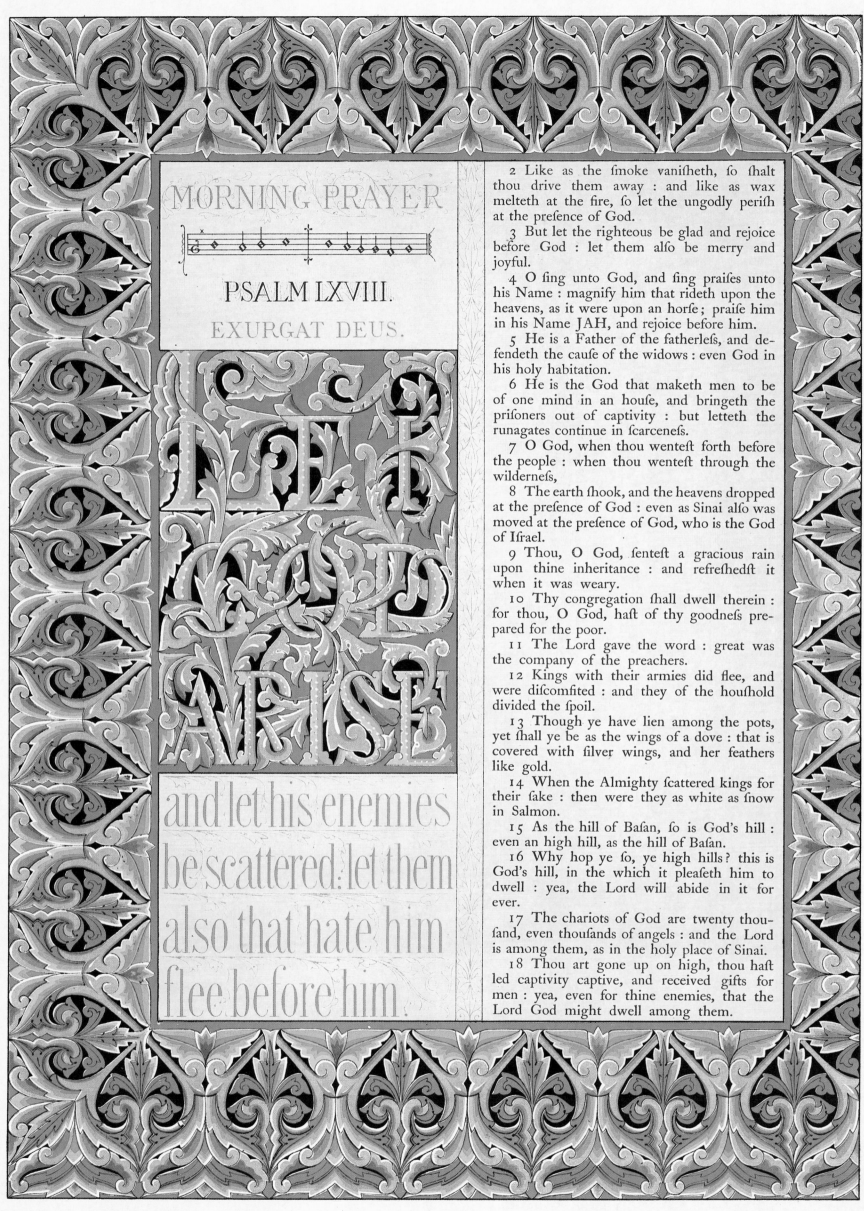

MORNING PRAYER

PSALM LXVIII.

EXURGAT DEUS.

LET GOD ARISE

and let his enemies be scattered: let them also that hate him flee before him.

2 Like as the smoke vanisheth, so shalt thou drive them away : and like as wax melteth at the fire, so let the ungodly perish at the presence of God.

3 But let the righteous be glad and rejoice before God : let them also be merry and joyful.

4 O sing unto God, and sing praises unto his Name : magnify him that rideth upon the heavens, as it were upon an horse; praise him in his Name JAH, and rejoice before him.

5 He is a Father of the fatherless, and defendeth the cause of the widows : even God in his holy habitation.

6 He is the God that maketh men to be of one mind in an house, and bringeth the prisoners out of captivity : but letteth the runagates continue in scarceness.

7 O God, when thou wentest forth before the people : when thou wentest through the wilderness,

8 The earth shook, and the heavens dropped at the presence of God : even as Sinai also was moved at the presence of God, who is the God of Israel.

9 Thou, O God, sentest a gracious rain upon thine inheritance : and refreshedst it when it was weary.

10 Thy congregation shall dwell therein : for thou, O God, hast of thy goodness prepared for the poor.

11 The Lord gave the word : great was the company of the preachers.

12 Kings with their armies did flee, and were discomfited : and they of the houshold divided the spoil.

13 Though ye have lien among the pots, yet shall ye be as the wings of a dove : that is covered with silver wings, and her feathers like gold.

14 When the Almighty scattered kings for their sake : then were they as white as snow in Salmon.

15 As the hill of Basan, so is God's hill : even an high hill, as the hill of Basan.

16 Why hop ye so, ye high hills? this is God's hill, in the which it pleaseth him to dwell : yea, the Lord will abide in it for ever.

17 The chariots of God are twenty thousand, even thousands of angels : and the Lord is among them, as in the holy place of Sinai.

18 Thou art gone up on high, thou hast led captivity captive, and received gifts for men : yea, even for thine enemies, that the Lord God might dwell among them.

19 Praifed be the Lord daily : even the God who helpeth us, and poureth his benefits upon us.

20 He is our God, even the God of whom cometh falvation : God is the Lord, by whom we efcape death.

21 God fhall wound the head of his enemies : and the hairy fcalp of fuch a one as goeth on ftill in his wickednefs.

22 The Lord hath faid, I will bring my people again, as I did from Bafan : mine own will I bring again, as I did fometime from the deep of the fea.

23 That thy foot may be dipped in the blood of thine enemies : and that the tongue of thy dogs may be red through the fame.

24 It is well feen, O God, how thou goeft : how thou, my God and King, goeft in the fanctuary.

25 The fingers go before, the minftrels follow after : in the midft are the damfels playing with the timbrels.

26 Give thanks, O Ifrael, unto God the Lord in the congregations : from the ground of the heart.

27 There is little Benjamin their ruler, and the princes of Judah their counfel : the princes of Zabulon, and the princes of Nephthali.

28 Thy God hath fent forth ftrength for thee : ftablifh the thing, O God, that thou haft wrought in us,

29 For thy temple's fake at Jerufalem : fo fhall kings bring prefents unto thee.

30 When the company of the fpear-men, and multitude of the mighty are fcattered abroad among the beafts of the people, fo that they humbly bring pieces of filver : and when he hath fcattered the people that delight in war ;

31 Then fhall the princes come out of Egypt : the Morians' land fhall foon ftretch out her hands unto God.

32 Sing unto God, O ye kingdoms of the earth : O fing praifes unto the Lord ;

33 Who fitteth in the heavens over all from the beginning : lo, he doth fend out his voice, yea, and that a mighty voice.

34 Afcribe ye the power to God over Ifrael : his worfhip, and ftrength is in the clouds.

35 O God, wonderful art thou in thy holy places : even the God of Ifrael ; he will give ftrength and power unto his people ; bleffed be God.

EVENING PRAYER

PSALM LXIX.

SALVUM ME FAC

AVE me, O God : for the waters are come in, even unto my foul.

2 I ftick faft in the deep mire, where no ground is : I am come into deep waters, fo that the floods run over me.

3 I am weary of crying ; my throat is dry : my fight faileth me for waiting fo long upon my God.

4 They that hate me without a caufe are more than the hairs of my head : they that are mine enemies, and would deftroy me guiltlefs, are mighty.

5 I paid them the things that I never took : God, thou knoweft my fimplenefs, and my faults are not hid from thee.

6 Let not them that truft in thee, O Lord God of hofts, be afhamed for my caufe : let not thofe that feek thee be confounded through me, O Lord God of Ifrael.

7 And why ? for thy fake have I fuffered reproof : fhame hath covered my face.

8 I am become a ftranger unto my brethren : even an alien unto my mother's children.

9 For the zeal of thine houfe hath even eaten me : and the rebukes of them that rebuked thee are fallen upon me.

10 I wept, and chaftened myfelf with fafting : and that was turned to my reproof.

11 I put on fackcloth alfo : and they jefted upon me.

12 They that fit in the gate fpeak againft me : and the drunkards make fongs upon me.

13 But, Lord, I make my prayer unto thee : in an acceptable time.

14 Hear me, O God, in the multitude of thy mercy : even in the truth of thy salvation.

15 Take me out of the mire, that I sink not : O let me be delivered from them that hate me, and out of the deep waters.

16 Let not the water-flood drown me, neither let the deep swallow me up : and let not the pit shut her mouth upon me.

17 Hear me, O Lord, for thy loving-kindness is comfortable : turn thee unto me according to the multitude of thy mercies.

18 And hide not thy face from thy servant, for I am in trouble : O haste thee, and hear me.

19 Draw nigh unto my soul, and save it : O deliver me, because of mine enemies.

20 Thou hast known my reproof, my shame, and my dishonour : mine adversaries are all in thy sight.

21 Thy rebuke hath broken my heart; I am full of heaviness : I looked for some to have pity on me, but there was no man, neither found I any to comfort me.

22 They gave me gall to eat : and when I was thirsty they gave me vinegar to drink.

23 Let their table be made a snare to take themselves withal : and let the things that should have been for their wealth be unto them an occasion of falling.

24 Let their eyes be blinded, that they see not : and ever bow thou down their backs.

25 Pour out thine indignation upon them : and let thy wrathful displeasure take hold of them.

26 Let their habitation be void : and no man to dwell in their tents.

27 For they persecute him whom thou hast smitten : and they talk how they may vex them whom thou hast wounded.

28 Let them fall from one wickedness to another : and not come into thy righteousness.

29 Let them be wiped out of the book of the living : and not be written among the righteous.

30 As for me, when I am poor and in heaviness : thy help, O God, shall lift me up.

31 I will praise the Name of God with a song : and magnify it with thanksgiving.

32 This also shall please the Lord : better than a bullock that hath horns and hoofs.

33 The humble shall consider this, and be glad : seek ye after God, and your soul shall live.

34 For the Lord heareth the poor : and despiseth not his prisoners.

35 Let heaven and earth praise him : the sea, and all that moveth therein.

36 For God will save Sion, and build the cities of Judah : that men may dwell there, and have it in possession.

37 The posterity also of his servants shall inherit it : and they that love his Name shall dwell therein.

Psalm LXX.
Deus in adjutorium.

HASTE thee, O God, to deliver me : make haste to help me, O Lord.

2 Let them be ashamed and confounded that seek after my soul : let them be turned backward and put to confusion that wish me evil.

3 Let them for their reward be soon brought to shame : that cry over me, There, there.

4 But let all those that seek thee be joyful and glad in thee : and let all such as delight in thy salvation say alway, The Lord be praised.

5 As for me, I am poor and in misery : haste thee unto me, O God.

6 Thou art my helper, and my redeemer : O Lord, make no long tarrying.

MORNING PRAYER

PSALM LXXI.

IN TE, DOMINE, SPERAVI.

IN thee, O Lord, have I put my trust, let me never be put to confusion : but rid me, and deliver me, in thy righteousness; incline thine ear unto me, and save me.

2 Be thou my strong hold, whereunto I may alway resort : thou hast promised to help

me, for thou art my houſe of defence, and my caſtle.

3 Deliver me, O my God, out of the hand of the ungodly : out of the hand of the unrighteous and cruel man.

4 For thou, O Lord God, art the thing that I long for : thou art my hope, even from my youth.

5 Through thee have I been holden up ever ſince I was born : thou art he that took me out of my mother's womb; my praiſe ſhall be always of thee.

6 I am become as it were a monſter unto many : but my ſure truſt is in thee.

7 O let my mouth be filled with thy praiſe : that I may ſing of thy glory and honour all the day long.

8 Caſt me not away in the time of age : forſake me not when my ſtrength faileth me.

9 For mine enemies ſpeak againſt me, and they that lay wait for my ſoul take their counſel together, ſaying : God hath forſaken him; perſecute him, and take him, for there is none to deliver him.

10 Go not far from me, O God : my God, haſte thee to help me.

11 Let them be confounded and periſh that are againſt my ſoul : let them be covered with ſhame and diſhonour that ſeek to do me evil.

12 As for me, I will patiently abide alway : and will praiſe thee more and more.

13 My mouth ſhall daily ſpeak of thy righteouſneſs and ſalvation : for I know no end thereof.

14 I will go forth in the ſtrength of the Lord God : and will make mention of thy righteouſneſs only.

15 Thou, O God, haſt taught me from my youth up until now : therefore will I tell of thy wondrous works.

16 Forſake me not, O God, in mine old age, when I am gray-headed : until I have ſhewed thy ſtrength unto this generation, and thy power to all them that are yet for to come.

17 Thy righteouſneſs, O God, is very high : and great things are they that thou haſt done; O God, who is like unto thee ?

18 O what great troubles and adverſities haſt thou ſhewed me ! and yet didſt thou turn and refreſh me : yea, and broughteſt me from the deep of the earth again.

19 Thou haſt brought me to great honour : and comforted me on every ſide.

20 Therefore will I praiſe thee and thy faithfulneſs, O God, playing upon an inſtrument of muſick : unto thee will I ſing upon the harp, O thou Holy One of Iſrael.

21 My lips will be fain when I ſing unto thee : and ſo will my ſoul whom thou haſt delivered.

22 My tongue alſo ſhall talk of thy righteouſneſs all the day long : for they are confounded and brought unto ſhame that ſeek to do me evil.

Psalm LXXII.

Deus, judicium.

IVE the King thy judgements, O God : and thy righteouſneſs unto the King's ſon.

2 Then ſhall he judge thy people according unto right : and defend the poor.

3 The mountains alſo ſhall bring peace : and the little hills righteouſneſs unto the people.

4 He ſhall keep the ſimple folk by their right : defend the children of the poor, and puniſh the wrong doer.

5 They ſhall fear thee, as long as the ſun and moon endureth : from one generation to another.

6 He ſhall come down like the rain into a fleece of wool : even as the drops that water the earth.

7 In his time ſhall the righteous flouriſh : yea, and abundance of peace, ſo long as the moon endureth.

8 His dominion ſhall be alſo from the one ſea to the other : and from the flood unto the world's end.

9 They that dwell in the wilderneſs ſhall kneel before him : his enemies ſhall lick the duſt.

10 The kings of Tharſis and of the iſles ſhall give preſents : the kings of Arabia and Saba ſhall bring gifts.

11 All kings ſhall fall down before him : all nations ſhall do him ſervice.

12 For he ſhall deliver the poor when he crieth : the needy alſo, and him that hath no helper.

13 He ſhall be favourable to the ſimple and needy : and ſhall preſerve the ſouls of the poor.

14 He ſhall deliver their ſouls from falſehood and wrong : and dear ſhall their blood be in his ſight.

15 He ſhall live, and unto him ſhall be given of the gold of Arabia : prayer ſhall be made ever unto him, and daily ſhall he be praiſed.

16 There shall be an heap of corn in the earth, high upon the hills : his fruit shall shake like Libanus, and shall be green in the city like grafs upon the earth.

17 His Name shall endure for ever; his Name shall remain under the sun among the posterities : which shall be blessed through him ; and all the heathen shall praise him.

18 Blessed be the Lord God, even the God of Israel : which only doeth wondrous things ;

19 And blessed be the Name of his Majesty for ever : and all the earth shall be filled with his Majesty.   Amen, Amen.

EVENING PRAYER

PSALM LXXIII.

QUAM BONUS ISRAEL!

RULY God is loving unto Israel : even unto such as are of a clean heart.

2 Neverthelefs, my feet were almoft gone : my treadings had well-nigh flipt.

3 And why ? I was grieved at the wicked : I do also fee the ungodly in fuch prosperity.

4 For they are in no peril of death : but are lufty and strong.

5 They come in no misfortune like other folk : neither are they plagued like other men.

6 And this is the caufe that they are fo holden with pride : and overwhelmed with cruelty.

7 Their eyes swell with fatnefs : and they do even what they luft.

8 They corrupt other, and speak of wicked blafphemy : their talking is againft the moft High.

9 For they stretch forth their mouth unto the heaven : and their tongue goeth through the world.

10 Therefore fall the people unto them : and thereout fuck they no fmall advantage.

11 Tufh, fay they, how should God perceive it : is there knowledge in the moft High ?

12 Lo, thefe are the ungodly, thefe profper in the world, and thefe have riches in poffeffion : and I faid, Then have I cleanfed my heart in vain, and wafhed mine hands in innocency.

13 All the day long have I been punifhed : and chaftened every morning.

14 Yea, and I had almoft faid even as they : but lo, then I should have condemned the generation of thy children.

15 Then thought I to underftand this : but it was too hard for me,

16 Until I went into the fanctuary of God : then underftood I the end of thefe men ;

17 Namely, how thou doft fet them in flippery places : and cafteft them down, and deftroyeft them.

18 Oh, how fuddenly do they confume : perifh, and come to a fearful end !

19 Yea, even like as a dream when one awaketh : fo fhalt thou make their image to vanifh out of the city.

20 Thus my heart was grieved : and it went even through my reins.

21 So foolifh was I, and ignorant : even as it were a beaft before thee.

22 Nevertheless, I am alway by thee : for thou haft holden me by my right hand.

23 Thou fhalt guide me with thy counfel : and after that receive me with glory.

24 Whom have I in heaven but thee : and there is none upon earth that I defire in comparison of thee.

25 My flefh and my heart faileth : but God is the ftrength of my heart, and my portion for ever.

26 For lo, they that forfake thee fhall perifh : thou haft deftroyed all them that commit fornication againft thee.

27 But it is good for me to hold me faft by God, to put my truft in the Lord God : and to fpeak of all thy works in the gates of the daughter of Sion.

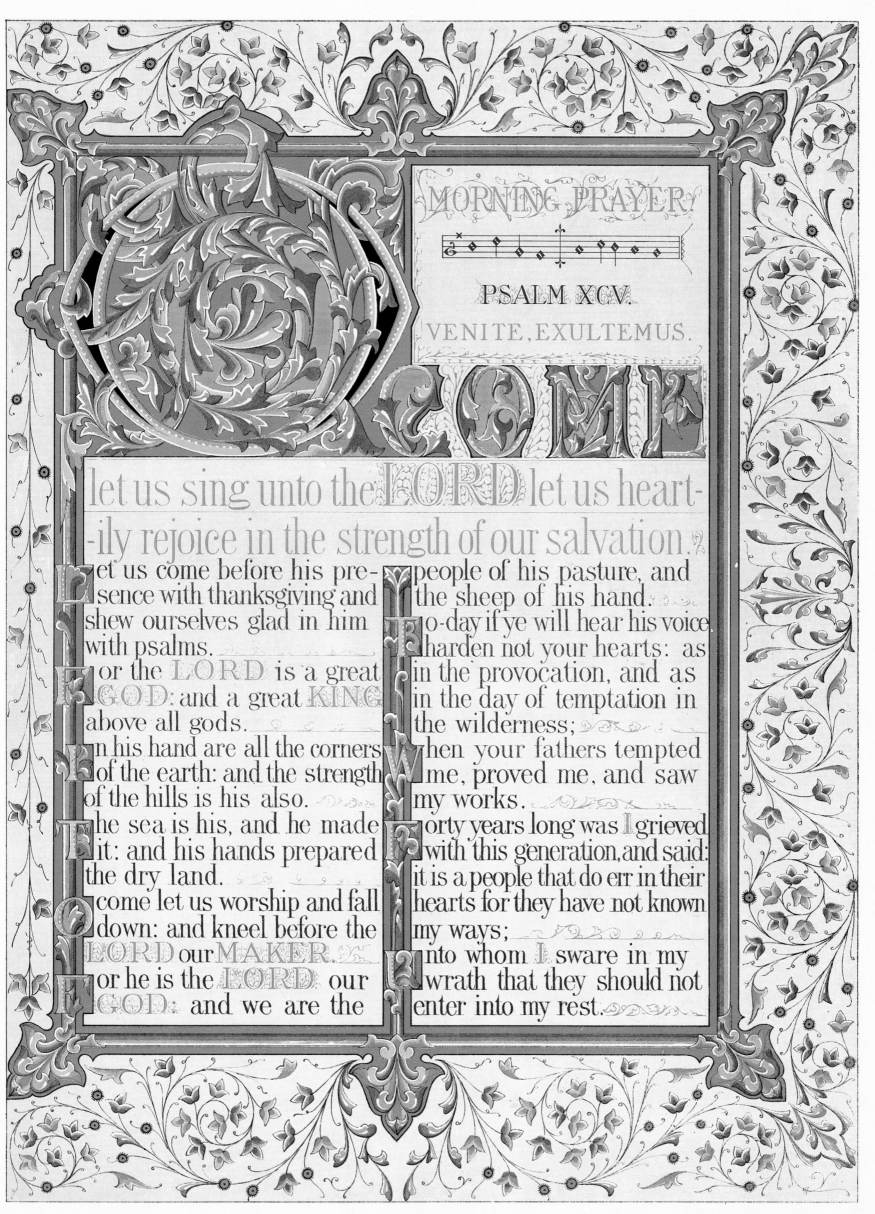

MORNING PRAYER.

PSALM XCV.

VENITE, EXULTEMUS.

O COME let us sing unto the LORD let us heart-ily rejoice in the strength of our salvation.

Let us come before his pre-sence with thanksgiving and shew ourselves glad in him with psalms.

For the LORD is a great GOD: and a great KING above all gods.

In his hand are all the corners of the earth: and the strength of the hills is his also.

The sea is his, and he made it: and his hands prepared the dry land.

O come let us worship and fall down: and kneel before the LORD our MAKER.

For he is the LORD our GOD: and we are the people of his pasture, and the sheep of his hand.

To-day if ye will hear his voice harden not your hearts: as in the provocation, and as in the day of temptation in the wilderness;

When your fathers tempted me, proved me, and saw my works.

Forty years long was I grieved with this generation, and said: it is a people that do err in their hearts for they have not known my ways;

Unto whom I sware in my wrath that they should not enter into my rest.

PSALM XCVI.

CANTATE DOMINO.

SING unto the Lord a new song : sing unto the Lord, all the whole earth.

2 Sing unto the Lord, and praise his Name : be telling of his salvation from day to day.

3 Declare his honour unto the heathen : and his wonders unto all people.

4 For the Lord is great, and cannot worthily be praised : he is more to be feared than all gods.

5 As for all the gods of the heathen, they are but idols : but it is the Lord that made the heavens.

6 Glory and worship are before him : power and honour are in his sanctuary.

7 Ascribe unto the Lord, O ye kindreds of the people : ascribe unto the Lord worship and power.

8 Ascribe unto the Lord the honour due unto his Name : bring presents, and come into his courts.

9 O worship the Lord in the beauty of holiness : let the whole earth stand in awe of him.

10 Tell it out among the heathen that the Lord is King : and that it is he who hath made the round world so fast that it cannot be moved; and how that he shall judge the people righteously.

11 Let the heavens rejoice, and let the earth be glad : let the sea make a noise, and all that therein is.

12 Let the field be joyful, and all that is in it : then shall all the trees of the wood rejoice before the Lord.

13 For he cometh, for he cometh to judge the earth : and with righteousness to judge the world, and the people with his truth.

PSALM XCVII.

Dominus regnavit.

THE Lord is King, the earth may be glad thereof : yea, the multitude of the isles may be glad thereof.

2 Clouds and darkness are round about him : righteousness and judgement are the habitation of his seat.

3 There shall go a fire before him : and burn up his enemies on every side.

4 His lightnings gave shine unto the world : the earth saw it, and was afraid.

5 The hills melted like wax at the presence of the Lord : at the presence of the Lord of the whole earth.

6 The heavens have declared his righteousness : and all the people have seen his glory.

7 Confounded be all they that worship carved images, and that delight in vain gods : worship him, all ye gods.

8 Sion heard of it, and rejoiced : and the daughters of Judah were glad, because of thy judgements, O Lord.

9 For thou, Lord, art higher than all that are in the earth : thou art exalted far above all gods.

10 O ye that love the Lord, see that ye hate the thing which is evil : the Lord preserveth the souls of his saints; he shall deliver them from the hand of the ungodly.

11 There is sprung up a light for the righteous : and joyful gladness for such as are true-hearted.

12 Rejoice in the Lord, ye righteous : and give thanks for a remembrance of his holiness.

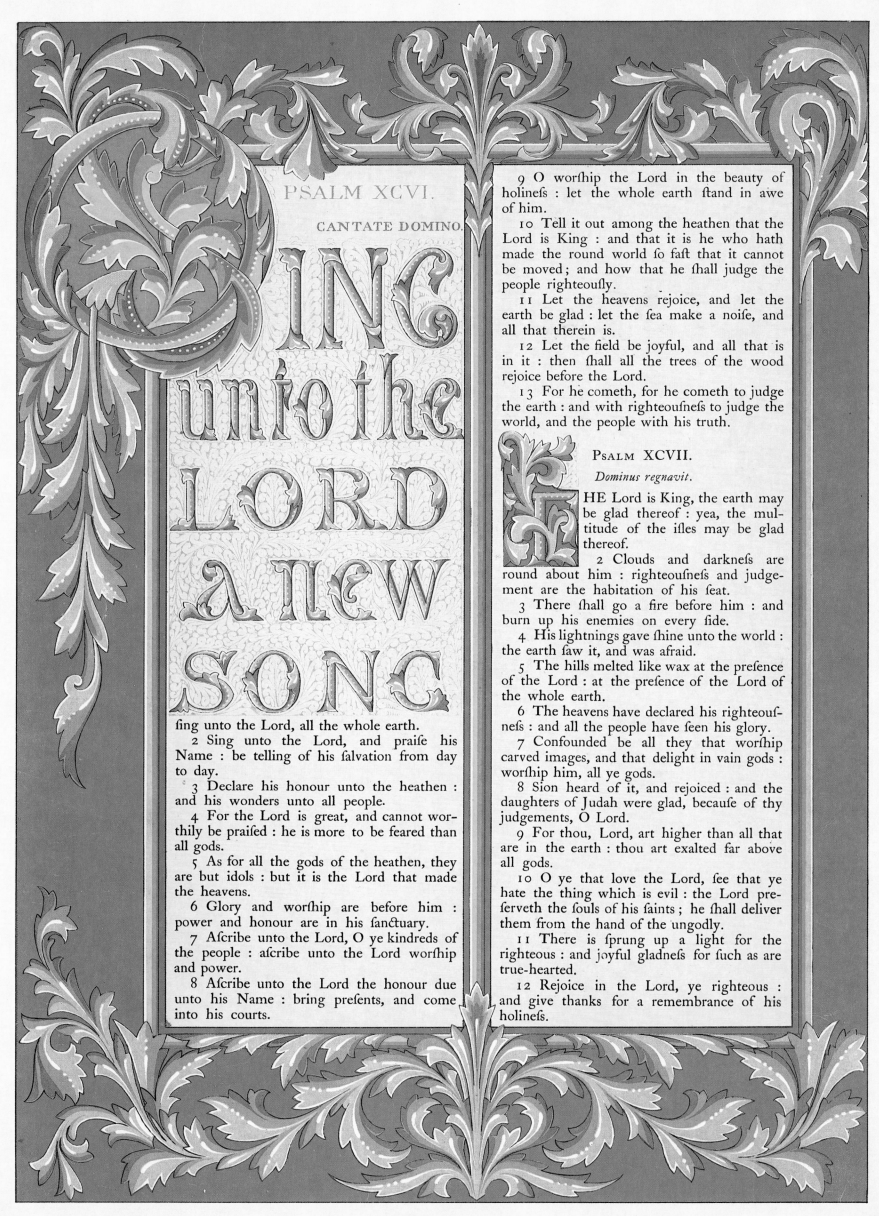

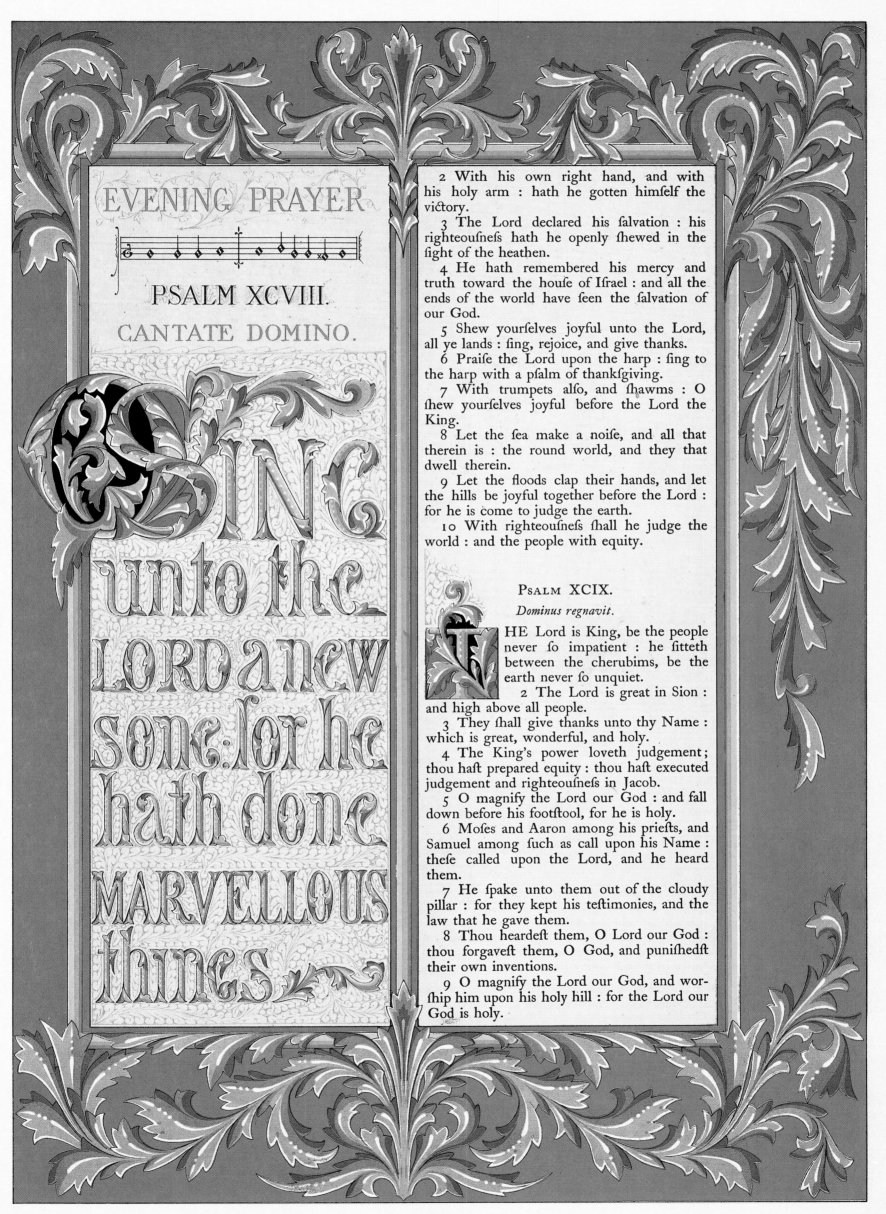

EVENING PRAYER

PSALM XCVIII.

CANTATE DOMINO.

SING unto the Lord a new song: for he hath done MARVELLOUS things

2 With his own right hand, and with his holy arm : hath he gotten himſelf the victory.

3 The Lord declared his ſalvation : his righteouſneſs hath he openly ſhewed in the ſight of the heathen.

4 He hath remembered his mercy and truth toward the houſe of Iſrael : and all the ends of the world have ſeen the ſalvation of our God.

5 Shew yourſelves joyful unto the Lord, all ye lands : ſing, rejoice, and give thanks.

6 Praiſe the Lord upon the harp : ſing to the harp with a pſalm of thankſgiving.

7 With trumpets alſo, and ſhawms : O ſhew yourſelves joyful before the Lord the King.

8 Let the ſea make a noiſe, and all that therein is : the round world, and they that dwell therein.

9 Let the floods clap their hands, and let the hills be joyful together before the Lord : for he is come to judge the earth.

10 With righteouſneſs ſhall he judge the world : and the people with equity.

PSALM XCIX.

Dominus regnavit.

THE Lord is King, be the people never ſo impatient : he ſitteth between the cherubims, be the earth never ſo unquiet.

2 The Lord is great in Sion : and high above all people.

3 They ſhall give thanks unto thy Name : which is great, wonderful, and holy.

4 The King's power loveth judgement; thou haſt prepared equity : thou haſt executed judgement and righteouſneſs in Jacob.

5 O magnify the Lord our God : and fall down before his footſtool, for he is holy.

6 Moſes and Aaron among his prieſts, and Samuel among ſuch as call upon his Name : theſe called upon the Lord, and he heard them.

7 He ſpake unto them out of the cloudy pillar : for they kept his teſtimonies, and the law that he gave them.

8 Thou heardeſt them, O Lord our God : thou forgaveſt them, O God, and puniſhedſt their own inventions.

9 O magnify the Lord our God, and worſhip him upon his holy hill : for the Lord our God is holy.

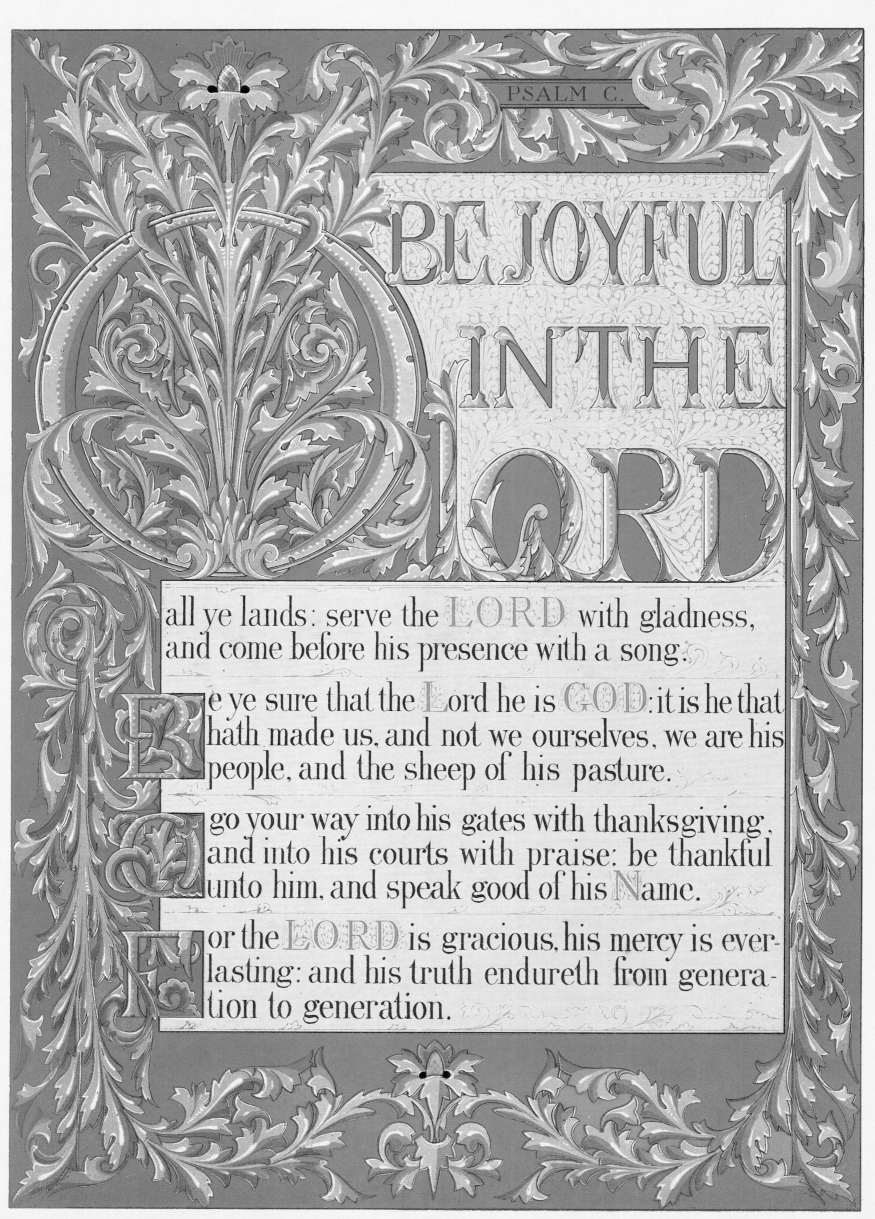

PSALM C.

BE JOYFUL IN THE LORD

all ye lands: serve the LORD with gladness, and come before his presence with a song.

e ye sure that the Lord he is GOD: it is he that hath made us, and not we ourselves, we are his people, and the sheep of his pasture.

go your way into his gates with thanksgiving, and into his courts with praise: be thankful unto him, and speak good of his Name.

or the LORD is gracious, his mercy is everlasting: and his truth endureth from generation to generation.

Psalm CI.

Misericordiam et judicium.

MY song shall be of mercy and judgement: unto thee, O Lord, will I sing.

2 O let me have understanding : in the way of godliness.

3 When wilt thou come unto me : I will walk in my house with a perfect heart.

4 I will take no wicked thing in hand ; I hate the sins of unfaithfulness : there shall no such cleave unto me.

5 A froward heart shall depart from me : I will not know a wicked person.

6 Whoso privily slandereth his neighbour : him will I destroy.

7 Whoso hath also a proud look and high stomach : I will not suffer him.

8 Mine eyes look upon such as are faithful in the land : that they may dwell with me.

9 Whoso leadeth a godly life : he shall be my servant.

10 There shall no deceitful person dwell in my house : he that telleth lies shall not tarry in my sight.

11 I shall soon destroy all the ungodly that are in the land : that I may root out all wicked doers from the city of the Lord.

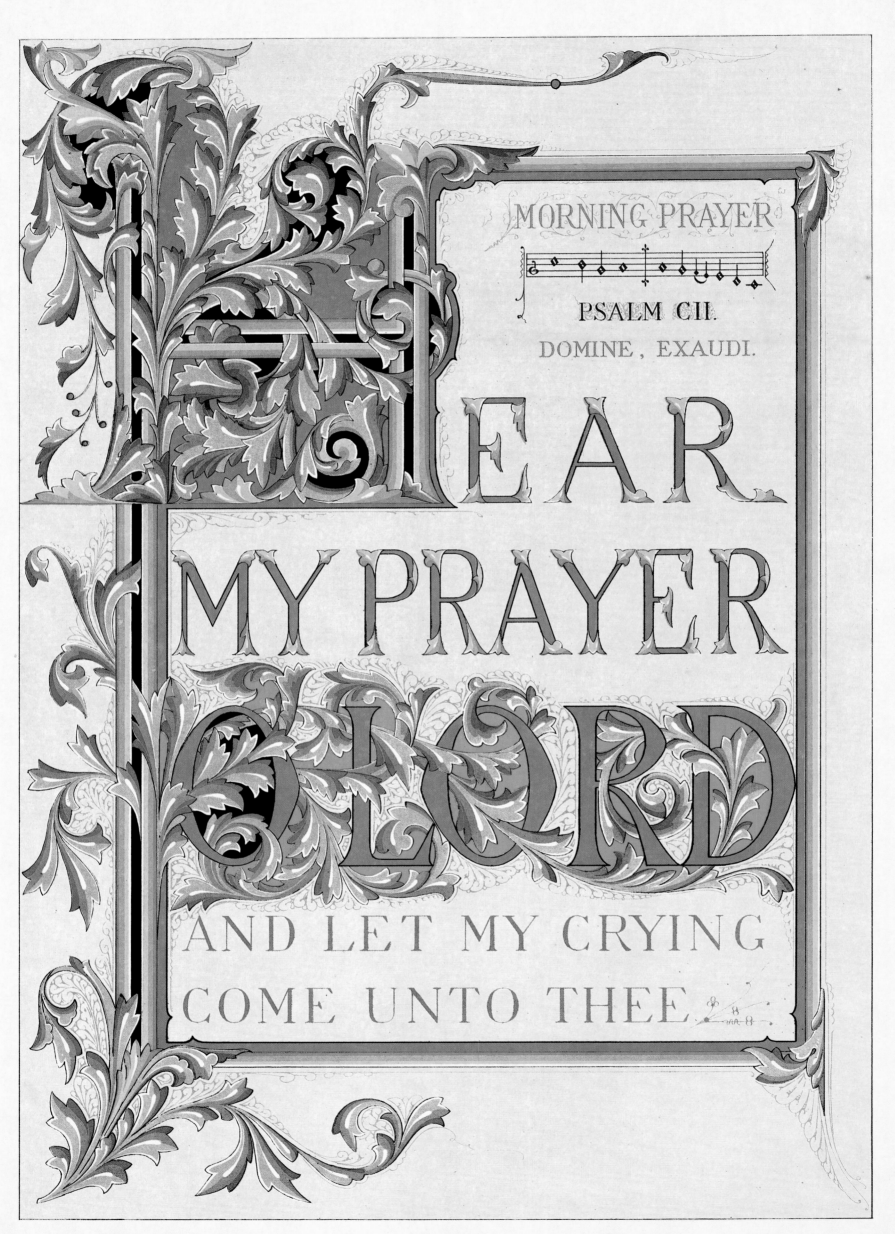

MORNING PRAYER

PSALM CII.

DOMINE, EXAUDI.

HEAR MY PRAYER O LORD AND LET MY CRYING COME UNTO THEE

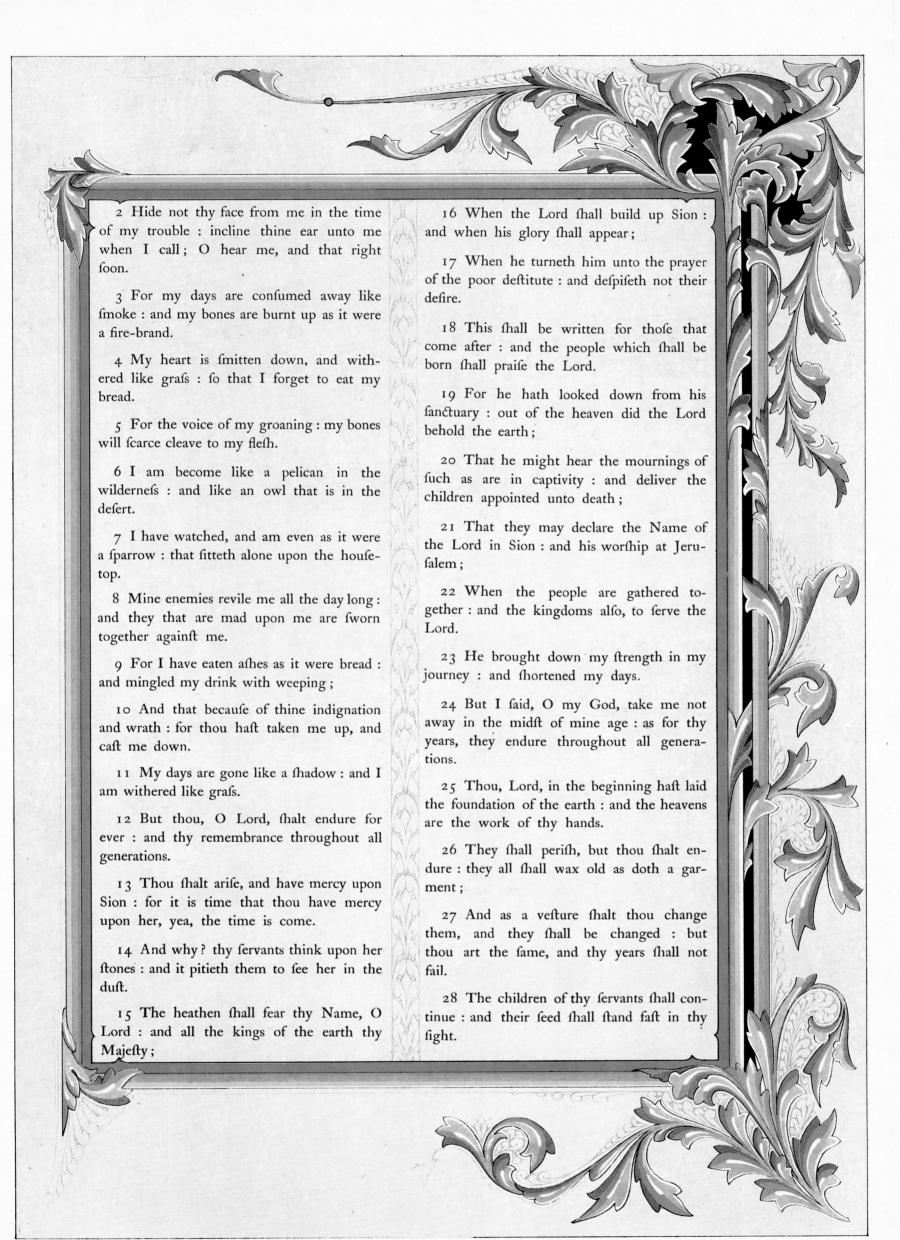

2 Hide not thy face from me in the time of my trouble : incline thine ear unto me when I call; O hear me, and that right foon.

3 For my days are confumed away like fmoke : and my bones are burnt up as it were a fire-brand.

4 My heart is fmitten down, and withered like grafs : fo that I forget to eat my bread.

5 For the voice of my groaning : my bones will fcarce cleave to my flefh.

6 I am become like a pelican in the wildernefs : and like an owl that is in the defert.

7 I have watched, and am even as it were a fparrow : that fitteth alone upon the houfetop.

8 Mine enemies revile me all the day long : and they that are mad upon me are fworn together againft me.

9 For I have eaten afhes as it were bread : and mingled my drink with weeping;

10 And that becaufe of thine indignation and wrath : for thou haft taken me up, and caft me down.

11 My days are gone like a fhadow : and I am withered like grafs.

12 But thou, O Lord, fhalt endure for ever : and thy remembrance throughout all generations.

13 Thou fhalt arife, and have mercy upon Sion : for it is time that thou have mercy upon her, yea, the time is come.

14 And why? thy fervants think upon her ftones : and it pitieth them to fee her in the duft.

15 The heathen fhall fear thy Name, O Lord : and all the kings of the earth thy Majefty;

16 When the Lord fhall build up Sion : and when his glory fhall appear;

17 When he turneth him unto the prayer of the poor deftitute : and defpifeth not their defire.

18 This fhall be written for thofe that come after : and the people which fhall be born fhall praife the Lord.

19 For he hath looked down from his fanctuary : out of the heaven did the Lord behold the earth;

20 That he might hear the mournings of fuch as are in captivity : and deliver the children appointed unto death;

21 That they may declare the Name of the Lord in Sion : and his worfhip at Jerufalem;

22 When the people are gathered together : and the kingdoms alfo, to ferve the Lord.

23 He brought down my ftrength in my journey : and fhortened my days.

24 But I faid, O my God, take me not away in the midft of mine age : as for thy years, they endure throughout all generations.

25 Thou, Lord, in the beginning haft laid the foundation of the earth : and the heavens are the work of thy hands.

26 They fhall perifh, but thou fhalt endure : they all fhall wax old as doth a garment;

27 And as a vefture fhalt thou change them, and they fhall be changed : but thou art the fame, and thy years fhall not fail.

28 The children of thy fervants fhall continue : and their feed fhall ftand faft in thy fight.

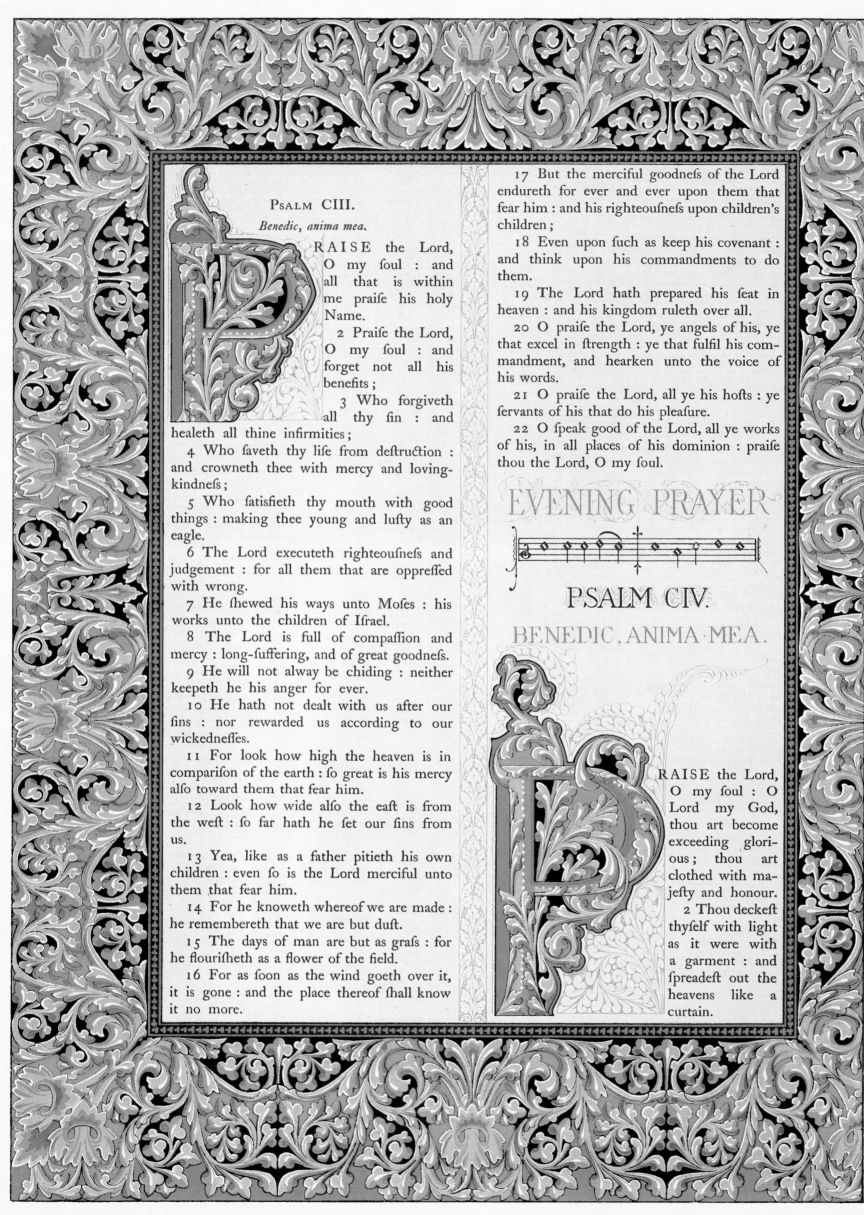

Psalm CIII.

Benedic, anima mea.

PRAISE the Lord, O my soul : and all that is within me praise his holy Name.

2 Praise the Lord, O my soul : and forget not all his benefits ;

3 Who forgiveth all thy sin : and healeth all thine infirmities ;

4 Who saveth thy life from destruction : and crowneth thee with mercy and loving-kindness ;

5 Who satisfieth thy mouth with good things : making thee young and lusty as an eagle.

6 The Lord executeth righteousness and judgement : for all them that are oppressed with wrong.

7 He shewed his ways unto Moses : his works unto the children of Israel.

8 The Lord is full of compassion and mercy : long-suffering, and of great goodness.

9 He will not alway be chiding : neither keepeth he his anger for ever.

10 He hath not dealt with us after our sins : nor rewarded us according to our wickednesses.

11 For look how high the heaven is in comparison of the earth : so great is his mercy also toward them that fear him.

12 Look how wide also the east is from the west : so far hath he set our sins from us.

13 Yea, like as a father pitieth his own children : even so is the Lord merciful unto them that fear him.

14 For he knoweth whereof we are made : he remembereth that we are but dust.

15 The days of man are but as grass : for he flourisheth as a flower of the field.

16 For as soon as the wind goeth over it, it is gone : and the place thereof shall know it no more.

17 But the merciful goodness of the Lord endureth for ever and ever upon them that fear him : and his righteousness upon children's children ;

18 Even upon such as keep his covenant : and think upon his commandments to do them.

19 The Lord hath prepared his seat in heaven : and his kingdom ruleth over all.

20 O praise the Lord, ye angels of his, ye that excel in strength : ye that fulfil his commandment, and hearken unto the voice of his words.

21 O praise the Lord, all ye his hosts : ye servants of his that do his pleasure.

22 O speak good of the Lord, all ye works of his, in all places of his dominion : praise thou the Lord, O my soul.

EVENING PRAYER

PSALM CIV.

BENEDIC, ANIMA MEA.

PRAISE the Lord, O my soul : O Lord my God, thou art become exceeding glorious ; thou art clothed with majesty and honour.

2 Thou deckest thyself with light as it were with a garment : and spreadest out the heavens like a curtain.

3 Who layeth the beams of his chambers in the waters : and maketh the clouds his chariot, and walketh upon the wings of the wind.

4 He maketh his angels fpirits : and his minifters a flaming fire.

5 He laid the foundations of the earth : that it never fhould move at any time.

6 Thou coveredft it with the deep like as with a garment : the waters ftand in the hills.

7 At thy rebuke they flee : at the voice of thy thunder they are afraid.

8 They go up as high as the hills, and down to the valleys beneath : even unto the place which thou haft appointed for them.

9 Thou haft fet them their bounds which they fhall not pafs : neither turn again to cover the earth.

10 He fendeth the fprings into the rivers : which run among the hills.

11 All beafts of the field drink thereof : and the wild affes quench their thirft.

12 Befide them fhall the fowls of the air have their habitation : and fing among the branches.

13 He watereth the hills from above : the earth is filled with the fruit of thy works.

14 He bringeth forth grafs for the cattle : and green herb for the fervice of men ;

15 That he may bring food out of the earth, and wine that maketh glad the heart of man : and oil to make him a cheerful countenance, and bread to ftrengthen man's heart.

16 The trees of the Lord alfo are full of fap : even the cedars of Libanus which he hath planted ;

17 Wherein the birds make their nefts : and the fir-trees are a dwelling for the ftork.

18 The high hills are a refuge for the wild goats : and fo are the ftony rocks for the conies.

19 He appointed the moon for certain feafons : and the fun knoweth his going down.

20 Thou makeft darknefs that it may be night : wherein all the beafts of the foreft do move.

21 The lions roaring after their prey : do feek their meat from God.

22 The fun arifeth, and they get them away together : and lay them down in their dens.

23 Man goeth forth to his work, and to his labour : until the evening.

24 O Lord, how manifold are thy works : in wifdom haft thou made them all ; the earth is full of thy riches.

25 So is the great and wide fea alfo : wherein are things creeping innumerable, both fmall and great beafts.

26 There go the fhips, and there is that Leviathan : whom thou haft made to take his paftime therein.

27 Thefe wait all upon thee : that thou mayeft give them meat in due feafon.

28 When thou giveft it them they gather it : and when thou openeft thy hand they are filled with good.

29 When thou hideft thy face they are troubled : when thou takeft away their breath they die, and are turned again to their duft.

30 When thou letteft thy breath go forth they fhall be made : and thou fhalt renew the face of the earth.

31 The glorious Majefty of the Lord fhall endure for ever : the Lord fhall rejoice in his works.

32 The earth fhall tremble at the look of him : if he do but touch the hills, they fhall fmoke.

33 I will fing unto the Lord as long as I live : I will praife my God while I have my being.

34 And fo fhall my words pleafe him : my joy fhall be in the Lord.

35 As for finners, they fhall be confumed out of the earth, and the ungodly fhall come to an end : praife thou the Lord, O my foul, praife the Lord.

MORNING PRAYER.

PSALM CV.
CONFITEMINI DOMINO.

GIVE thanks unto the Lord, and call upon his Name : tell the people what things he hath done.

2 O let your fongs be of him, and praife him : and let your talking be of all his wondrous works.

3 Rejoice in his holy Name : let the heart of them rejoice that feek the Lord.

4 Seek the Lord and his ftrength : feek his face evermore.

5 Remember the marvellous works that he hath done : his wonders, and the judgements of his mouth,

6 O ye feed of Abraham his fervant : ye children of Jacob his chofen.

7 He is the Lord our God : his judgements are in all the world.

8 He hath been alway mindful of his covenant and promife : that he made to a thoufand generations ;

9 Even the covenant that he made with Abraham : and the oath that he fware unto Ifaac ;

10 And appointed the fame unto Jacob for a law : and to Ifrael for an everlafting teftament ;

11 Saying, Unto thee will I give the land of Canaan : the lot of your inheritance ;

12 When there were yet but a few of them : and they ftrangers in the land ;

13 What time as they went from one nation to another : from one kingdom to another people ;

14 He fuffered no man to do them wrong : but reproved even kings for their fakes ;

15 Touch not mine Anointed : and do my prophets no harm.

16 Moreover, he called for a dearth upon the land : and deftroyed all the provifion of bread.

17 But he had fent a man before them : even Jofeph, who was fold to be a bond-fervant ;

18 Whofe feet they hurt in the ftocks : the iron entered into his foul ;

19 Until the time came that his caufe was known : the word of the Lord tried him.

20 The king fent, and delivered him : the prince of the people let him go free.

21 He made him lord alfo of his houfe : and ruler of all his fubftance ;

22 That he might inform his princes after his will : and teach his fenators wifdom.

23 Ifrael alfo came into Egypt : and Jacob was a ftranger in the land of Ham.

24 And he increafed his people exceedingly : and made them ftronger than their enemies ;

25 Whofe heart turned fo, that they hated his people : and dealt untruly with his fervants.

26 Then fent he Mofes his fervant : and Aaron whom he had chofen.

27 And thefe fhewed his tokens among them : and wonders in the land of Ham.

28 He fent darknefs, and it was dark : and they were not obedient unto his word.

29 He turned their waters into blood : and flew their fifh.

30 Their land brought forth frogs : yea, even in their kings' chambers.

31 He fpake the word, and there came all manner of flies : and lice in all their quarters.

32 He gave them hail-ftones for rain : and flames of fire in their land.

33 He fmote their vines alfo and fig-trees : and deftroyed the trees that were in their coafts.

34 He fpake the word, and the grafshoppers came, and caterpillars innumerable : and did eat up all the grafs in their land, and devoured the fruit of their ground.

35 He fmote all the firft-born in their land : even the chief of all their ftrength.

36 He brought them forth also with silver and gold : there was not one feeble person among their tribes.

37 Egypt was glad at their departing : for they were afraid of them.

38 He spread out a cloud to be a covering : and fire to give light in the night-season.

39 At their desire he brought quails : and he filled them with the bread of heaven.

40 He opened the rock of stone, and the waters flowed out : so that rivers ran in the dry places.

41 For why? he remembered his holy promise : and Abraham his servant.

42 And he brought forth his people with joy : and his chosen with gladness ;

43 And gave them the lands of the heathen : and they took the labours of the people in possession ;

44 That they might keep his statutes : and observe his laws.

EVENING PRAYER

PSALM CVI.

CONFITEMINI DOMINO

GIVE thanks unto the Lord, for he is gracious : and his mercy endureth for ever.

2 Who can express the noble acts of the Lord : or shew forth all his praise ?

3 Blessed are they that alway keep judgement : and do righteousness.

4 Remember me, O Lord, according to the favour that thou bearest unto thy people : O visit me with thy salvation ;

5 That I may see the felicity of thy chosen : and rejoice in the gladness of thy people, and give thanks with thine inheritance.

6 We have sinned with our fathers : we have done amiss, and dealt wickedly.

7 Our fathers regarded not thy wonders in Egypt, neither kept they thy great goodness in remembrance : but were disobedient at the sea, even at the Red sea.

8 Nevertheless, he helped them for his Name's sake : that he might make his power to be known.

9 He rebuked the Red sea also, and it was dried up : so he led them through the deep, as through a wilderness.

10 And he saved them from the adversary's hand : and delivered them from the hand of the enemy.

11 As for those that troubled them, the waters overwhelmed them : there was not one of them left.

12 Then believed they his words : and sang praise unto him.

13 But within a while they forgat his works : and would not abide his counsel.

14 But lust came upon them in the wilderness : and they tempted God in the desert.

15 And he gave them their desire : and sent leanness withal into their soul.

16 They angered Moses also in the tents : and Aaron the saint of the Lord.

17 So the earth opened, and swallowed up Dathan : and covered the congregation of Abiram.

18 And the fire was kindled in their company : the flame burnt up the ungodly.

19 They made a calf in Horeb : and worshipped the molten image.

20 Thus they turned their glory : into the similitude of a calf that eateth hay.

21 And they forgat God their Saviour : who had done so great things in Egypt ;

22 Wondrous works in the land of Ham : and fearful things by the Red sea.

23 So he said, he would have destroyed them, had not Moses his chosen stood before him in the gap : to turn away his wrathful indignation, lest he should destroy them.

24 Yea, they thought scorn of that pleasant land : and gave no credence unto his word ;

25 But murmured in their tents : and hearkened not unto the voice of the Lord.

26 Then lift he up his hand against them : to overthrow them in the wilderness ;

27 To cast out their seed among the nations : and to scatter them in the lands.

28 They joined themfelves unto Baal-peor : and ate the offerings of the dead.

29 Thus they provoked him to anger with their own inventions : and the plague was great among them.

30 Then ftood up Phinees and prayed : and fo the plague ceafed.

31 And that was counted unto him for righteoufnefs : among all pofterities for ever-more.

32 They angered him alfo at the waters of ftrife : fo that he punifhed Mofes for their fakes ;

33 Becaufe they provoked his fpirit : fo that he fpake unadvifedly with his lips.

34 Neither deftroyed they the heathen : as the Lord commanded them ;

35 But were mingled among the heathen : and learned their works.

36 Infomuch that they worfhipped their idols, which turned to their own decay : yea, they offered their fons and their daughters unto devils ;

37 And fhed innocent blood, even the blood of their fons and of their daughters : whom they offered unto the idols of Canaan ; and the land was defiled with blood.

38 Thus were they ftained with their own works : and went a whoring with their own inventions.

39 Therefore was the wrath of the Lord kindled againft his people : infomuch that he abhorred his own inheritance.

40 And he gave them over into the hand of the heathen : and they that hated them were lords over them.

41 Their enemies oppreffed them : and had them in fubjection.

42 Many a time did he deliver them : but they rebelled againft him with their own inventions, and were brought down in their wickednefs.

43 Neverthelefs, when he faw their ad-verfity : he heard their complaint.

44 He thought upon his covenant, and pitied them, according unto the multitude of his mercies : yea, he made all thofe that led them away captive to pity them.

45 Deliver us, O Lord our God, and gather us from among the heathen : that we may give thanks unto thy holy Name, and make our boaft of thy praife.

46 Bleffed be the Lord God of Ifrael from everlafting, and world without end : and let all the people fay, Amen.

MORNING PRAYER

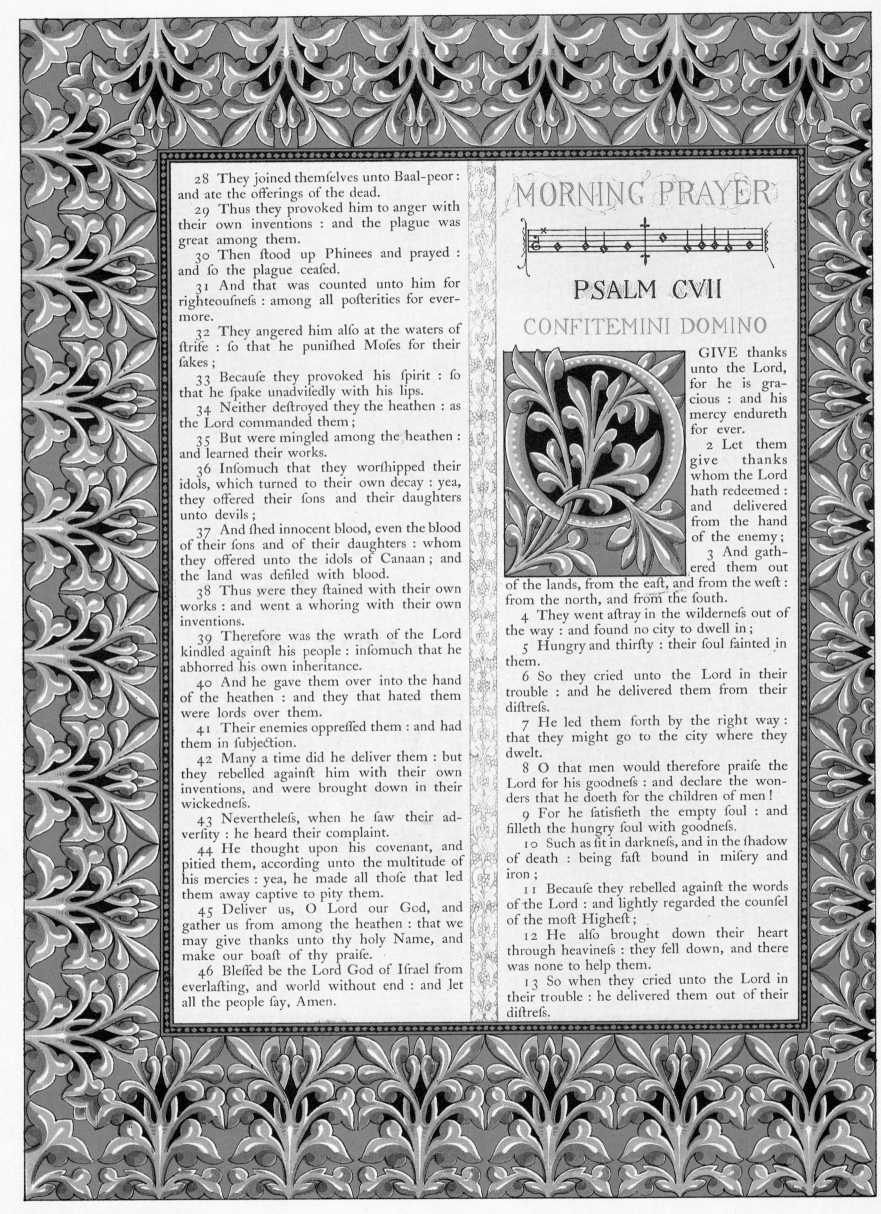

PSALM CVII

CONFITEMINI DOMINO

GIVE thanks unto the Lord, for he is gracious : and his mercy endureth for ever.

2 Let them give thanks whom the Lord hath redeemed : and delivered from the hand of the enemy ;

3 And gathered them out of the lands, from the eaft, and from the weft : from the north, and from the fouth.

4 They went aftray in the wildernefs out of the way : and found no city to dwell in ;

5 Hungry and thirfty : their foul fainted in them.

6 So they cried unto the Lord in their trouble : and he delivered them from their diftrefs.

7 He led them forth by the right way : that they might go to the city where they dwelt.

8 O that men would therefore praife the Lord for his goodnefs : and declare the wonders that he doeth for the children of men !

9 For he fatisfieth the empty foul : and filleth the hungry foul with goodnefs.

10 Such as fit in darknefs, and in the fhadow of death : being faft bound in mifery and iron ;

11 Becaufe they rebelled againft the words of the Lord : and lightly regarded the counfel of the moft Higheft ;

12 He alfo brought down their heart through heavinefs : they fell down, and there was none to help them.

13 So when they cried unto the Lord in their trouble : he delivered them out of their diftrefs.

14 For he brought them out of darkneſs, and out of the ſhadow of death : and brake their bonds in ſunder.

15 O that men would therefore praiſe the Lord for his goodneſs : and declare the wonders that he doeth for the children of men!

16 For he hath broken the gates of braſs : and ſmitten the bars of iron in ſunder.

17 Fooliſh men are plagued for their offence : and becauſe of their wickedneſs.

18 Their ſoul abhorred all manner of meat : and they were even hard at death's door.

19 So when they cried unto the Lord in their trouble : he delivered them out of their diſtreſs.

20 He ſent his word, and healed them : and they were ſaved from their deſtruction.

21 O that men would therefore praiſe the Lord for his goodneſs : and declare the wonders that he doeth for the children of men!

22 That they would offer unto him the ſacrifice of thankſgiving : and tell out his works with gladneſs!

23 They that go down to the ſea in ſhips : and occupy their buſineſs in great waters ;

24 Theſe men ſee the works of the Lord : and his wonders in the deep.

25 For at his word the ſtormy wind ariſeth : which lifteth up the waves thereof.

26 They are carried up to the heaven, and down again to the deep : their ſoul melteth away becauſe of the trouble.

27 They reel to and fro, and ſtagger like a drunken man : and are at their wit's end.

28 So when they cry unto the Lord in their trouble : he delivereth them out of their diſtreſs.

29 For he maketh the ſtorm to ceaſe : ſo that the waves thereof are ſtill.

30 Then are they glad, becauſe they are at reſt : and ſo he bringeth them unto the haven where they would be.

31 O that men would therefore praiſe the Lord for his goodneſs : and declare the wonders that he doeth for the children of men!

32 That they would exalt him alſo in the congregation of the people : and praiſe him in the ſeat of the elders !

33 Who turneth the floods into a wilderneſs : and drieth up the water-ſprings.

34 A fruitful land maketh he barren : for the wickedneſs of them that dwell therein.

35 Again, he maketh the wilderneſs a ſtanding water : and water-ſprings of a dry ground.

36 And there he ſetteth the hungry : that they may build them a city to dwell in ;

37 That they may ſow their land, and plant vineyards : to yield them fruits of increaſe.

38 He bleſſeth them, ſo that they multiply exceedingly : and ſuffereth not their cattle to decreaſe.

39 And again, when they are miniſhed, and brought low : through oppreſſion, through any plague, or trouble ;

40 Though he ſuffer them to be evil intreated through tyrants : and let them wander out of the way in the wilderneſs ;

41 Yet helpeth he the poor out of miſery : and maketh him houſholds like a flock of ſheep.

42 The righteous will conſider this, and rejoice : and the mouth of all wickedneſs ſhall be ſtopped.

43 Whoſo is wiſe will ponder theſe things : and they ſhall underſtand the loving-kindneſs of the Lord.

EVENING PRAYER

PSALM CVIII.

PARATUM COR MEUM

GOD, my heart is ready, my heart is ready : I will ſing and give praiſe with the beſt member that I have.

2 Awake, thou lute, and harp : I myſelf will awake right early.

3 I will give thanks unto thee, O Lord, among the people : I will ſing praiſes unto thee among the nations.

4 For thy mercy is greater than the heavens ; and thy truth reacheth unto the clouds.

5 Set up thyſelf, O God, above the heavens : and thy glory above all the earth.

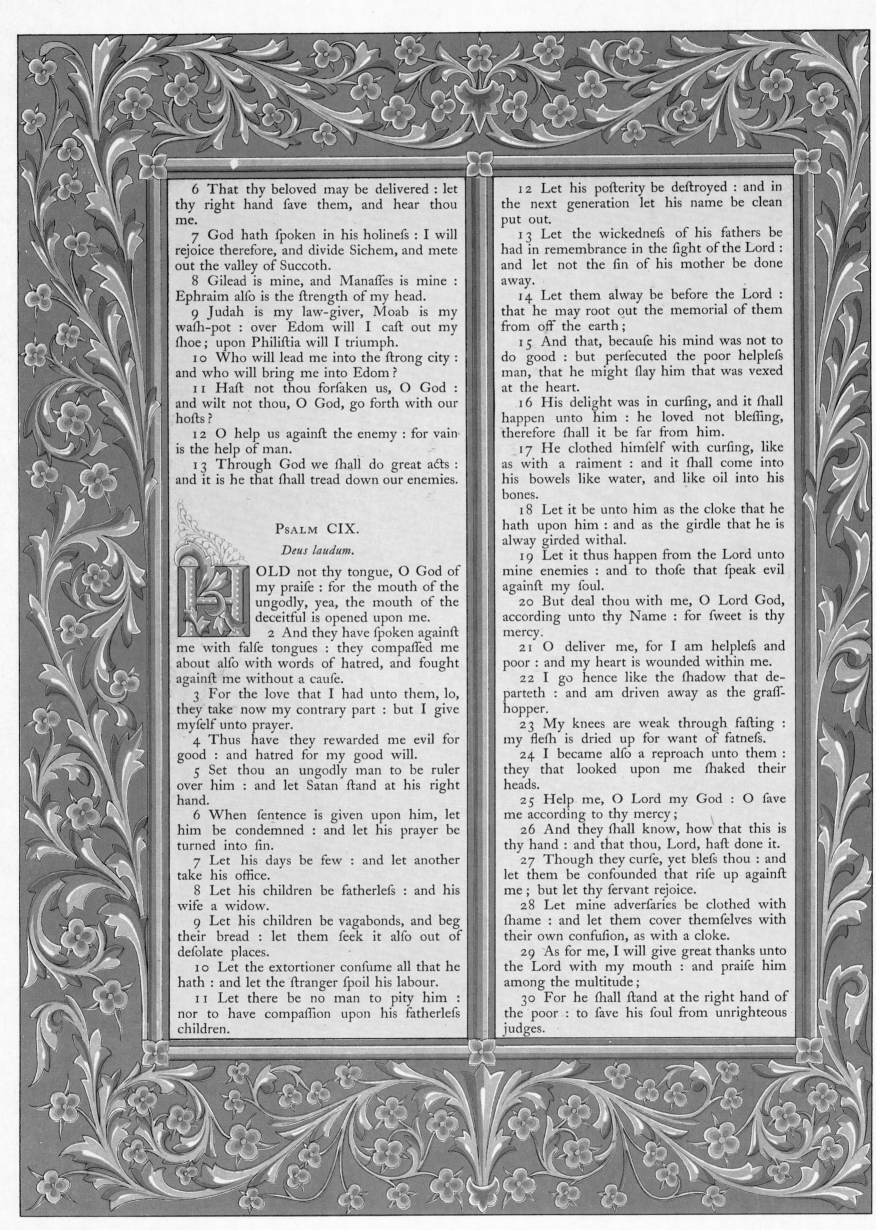

6 That thy beloved may be delivered : let thy right hand fave them, and hear thou me.

7 God hath fpoken in his holinefs : I will rejoice therefore, and divide Sichem, and mete out the valley of Succoth.

8 Gilead is mine, and Manaſſes is mine : Ephraim alſo is the ſtrength of my head.

9 Judah is my law-giver, Moab is my waſh-pot : over Edom will I caſt out my ſhoe; upon Philiſtia will I triumph.

10 Who will lead me into the ſtrong city : and who will bring me into Edom?

11 Haſt not thou forſaken us, O God : and wilt not thou, O God, go forth with our hoſts?

12 O help us againſt the enemy : for vain is the help of man.

13 Through God we ſhall do great acts : and it is he that ſhall tread down our enemies.

PSALM CIX.

Deus laudum.

HOLD not thy tongue, O God of my praiſe : for the mouth of the ungodly, yea, the mouth of the deceitful is opened upon me.

2 And they have ſpoken againſt me with falſe tongues : they compaſſed me about alſo with words of hatred, and fought againſt me without a cauſe.

3 For the love that I had unto them, lo, they take now my contrary part : but I give myſelf unto prayer.

4 Thus have they rewarded me evil for good : and hatred for my good will.

5 Set thou an ungodly man to be ruler over him : and let Satan ſtand at his right hand.

6 When ſentence is given upon him, let him be condemned : and let his prayer be turned into ſin.

7 Let his days be few : and let another take his office.

8 Let his children be fatherleſs : and his wife a widow.

9 Let his children be vagabonds, and beg their bread : let them ſeek it alſo out of deſolate places.

10 Let the extortioner conſume all that he hath : and let the ſtranger ſpoil his labour.

11 Let there be no man to pity him : nor to have compaſſion upon his fatherleſs children.

12 Let his poſterity be deſtroyed : and in the next generation let his name be clean put out.

13 Let the wickedneſs of his fathers be had in remembrance in the ſight of the Lord : and let not the ſin of his mother be done away.

14 Let them alway be before the Lord : that he may root out the memorial of them from off the earth;

15 And that, becauſe his mind was not to do good : but perſecuted the poor helpleſs man, that he might ſlay him that was vexed at the heart.

16 His delight was in curſing, and it ſhall happen unto him : he loved not bleſſing, therefore ſhall it be far from him.

17 He clothed himſelf with curſing, like as with a raiment : and it ſhall come into his bowels like water, and like oil into his bones.

18 Let it be unto him as the cloke that he hath upon him : and as the girdle that he is alway girded withal.

19 Let it thus happen from the Lord unto mine enemies : and to thoſe that ſpeak evil againſt my ſoul.

20 But deal thou with me, O Lord God, according unto thy Name : for ſweet is thy mercy.

21 O deliver me, for I am helpleſs and poor : and my heart is wounded within me.

22 I go hence like the ſhadow that departeth : and am driven away as the graſſhopper.

23 My knees are weak through faſting : my fleſh is dried up for want of fatneſs.

24 I became alſo a reproach unto them : they that looked upon me ſhaked their heads.

25 Help me, O Lord my God : O ſave me according to thy mercy;

26 And they ſhall know, how that this is thy hand : and that thou, Lord, haſt done it.

27 Though they curſe, yet bleſs thou : and let them be confounded that riſe up againſt me; but let thy ſervant rejoice.

28 Let mine adverſaries be clothed with ſhame : and let them cover themſelves with their own confuſion, as with a cloke.

29 As for me, I will give great thanks unto the Lord with my mouth : and praiſe him among the multitude;

30 For he ſhall ſtand at the right hand of the poor : to ſave his ſoul from unrighteous judges.

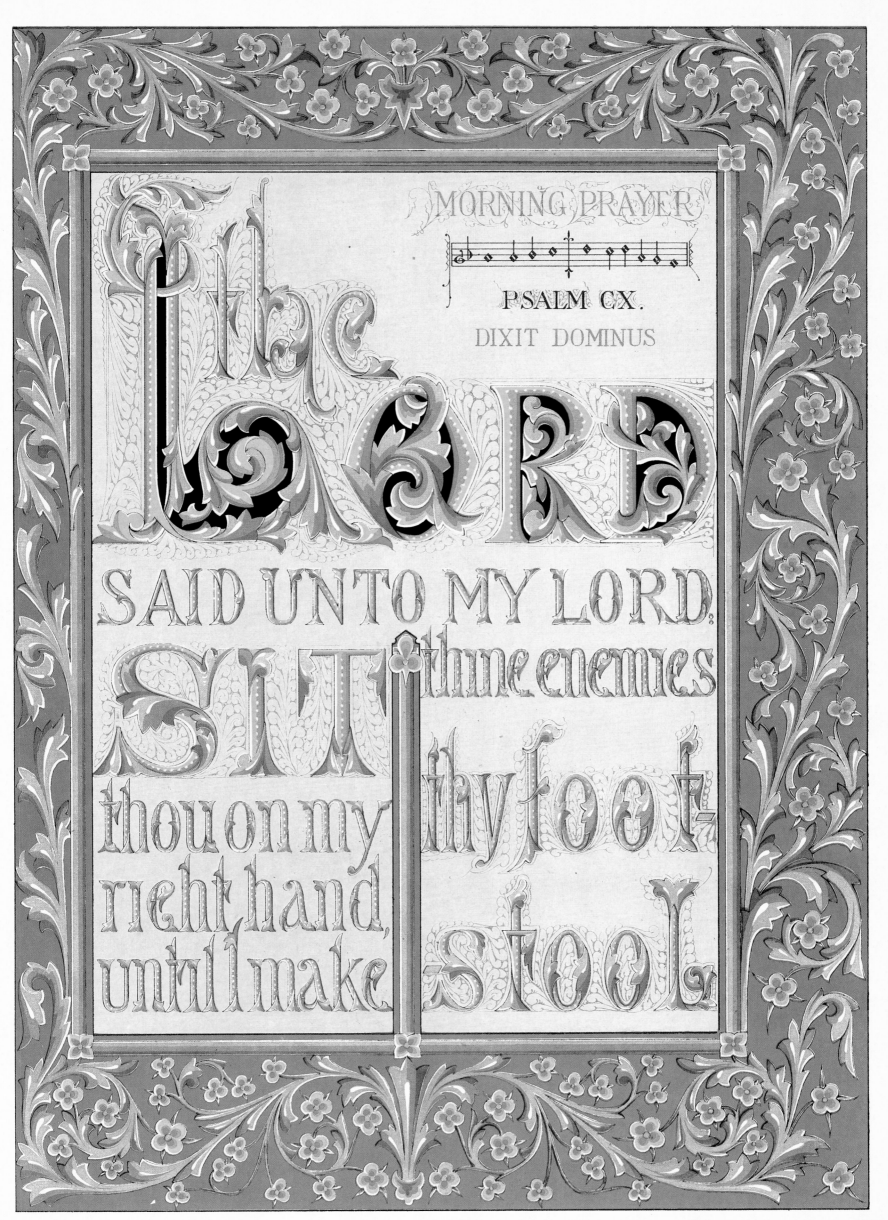

MORNING PRAYER

PSALM CX.

DIXIT DOMINUS

The LORD SAID UNTO MY LORD. SIT thou on my right hand, until I make thine enemies thy footstool.

2 The Lord ſhall ſend the rod of thy power out of Sion : be thou ruler, even in the midſt among thine enemies.

3 In the day of thy power ſhall the people offer thee free-will offerings with an holy worſhip : the dew of thy birth is of the womb of the morning.

4 The Lord ſware, and will not repent : Thou art a Prieſt for ever after the order of Melchiſedech.

5 The Lord upon thy right hand : ſhall wound even kings in the day of his wrath.

6 He ſhall judge among the heathen ; he ſhall fill the places with the dead bodies : and ſmite in ſunder the heads over divers countries.

7 He ſhall drink of the brook in the way : therefore ſhall he lift up his head.

Psalm CXI.

Confitebor tibi.

I WILL give thanks unto the Lord with my whole heart : ſecretly among the faithful, and in the congregation.

2 The works of the Lord are great : ſought out of all them that have pleaſure therein.

3 His work is worthy to be praiſed, and had in honour : and his righteouſneſs endureth for ever.

4 The merciful and gracious Lord hath ſo done his marvellous works : that they ought to be had in remembrance.

5 He hath given meat unto them that fear him : he ſhall ever be mindful of his covenant.

6 He hath ſhewed his people the power of his works : that he may give them the heritage of the heathen.

7 The works of his hands are verity and judgement : all his commandments are true.

8 They ſtand faſt for ever and ever : and are done in truth and equity.

9 He ſent redemption unto his people : he hath commanded his covenant for ever ; holy and reverend is his Name.

10 The fear of the Lord is the beginning of wiſdom : a good underſtanding have all they that do thereafter ; the praiſe of it endureth for ever.

Psalm CXII.

Beatus vir.

BLESSED is the man that feareth the Lord : he hath great delight in his commandments.

2 His ſeed ſhall be mighty upon earth : the generation of the faithful ſhall be bleſſed.

3 Riches and plenteouſneſs ſhall be in his houſe : and his righteouſneſs endureth for ever.

4 Unto the godly there ariſeth up light in the darkneſs : he is merciful, loving, and righteous.

5 A good man is merciful, and lendeth : and will guide his words with diſcretion.

6 For he ſhall never be moved : and the righteous ſhall be had in everlaſting remembrance.

7 He will not be afraid of any evil tidings : for his heart ſtandeth faſt, and believeth in the Lord.

8 His heart is eſtabliſhed, and will not ſhrink : until he ſee his deſire upon his enemies.

9 He hath diſperſed abroad, and given to the poor : and his righteouſneſs remaineth for ever ; his horn ſhall be exalted with honour.

10 The ungodly ſhall ſee it, and it ſhall grieve him : he ſhall gnaſh with his teeth, and conſume away ; the deſire of the ungodly ſhall periſh.

Psalm CXIII.

Laudate, pueri.

PRAISE the Lord, ye ſervants : O praiſe the Name of the Lord.

2 Bleſſed be the Name of the Lord : from this time forth for evermore.

3 The Lord's Name is praiſed : from the riſing up of the ſun unto the going down of the ſame.

4 The Lord is high above all heathen : and his glory above the heavens.

5 Who is like unto the Lord our God, that hath his dwelling ſo high : and yet humbleth himſelf to behold the things that are in heaven and earth ?

6 He taketh up the ſimple out of the duſt : and lifteth the poor out of the mire ;

7 That he may ſet him with the princes : even with the princes of his people.

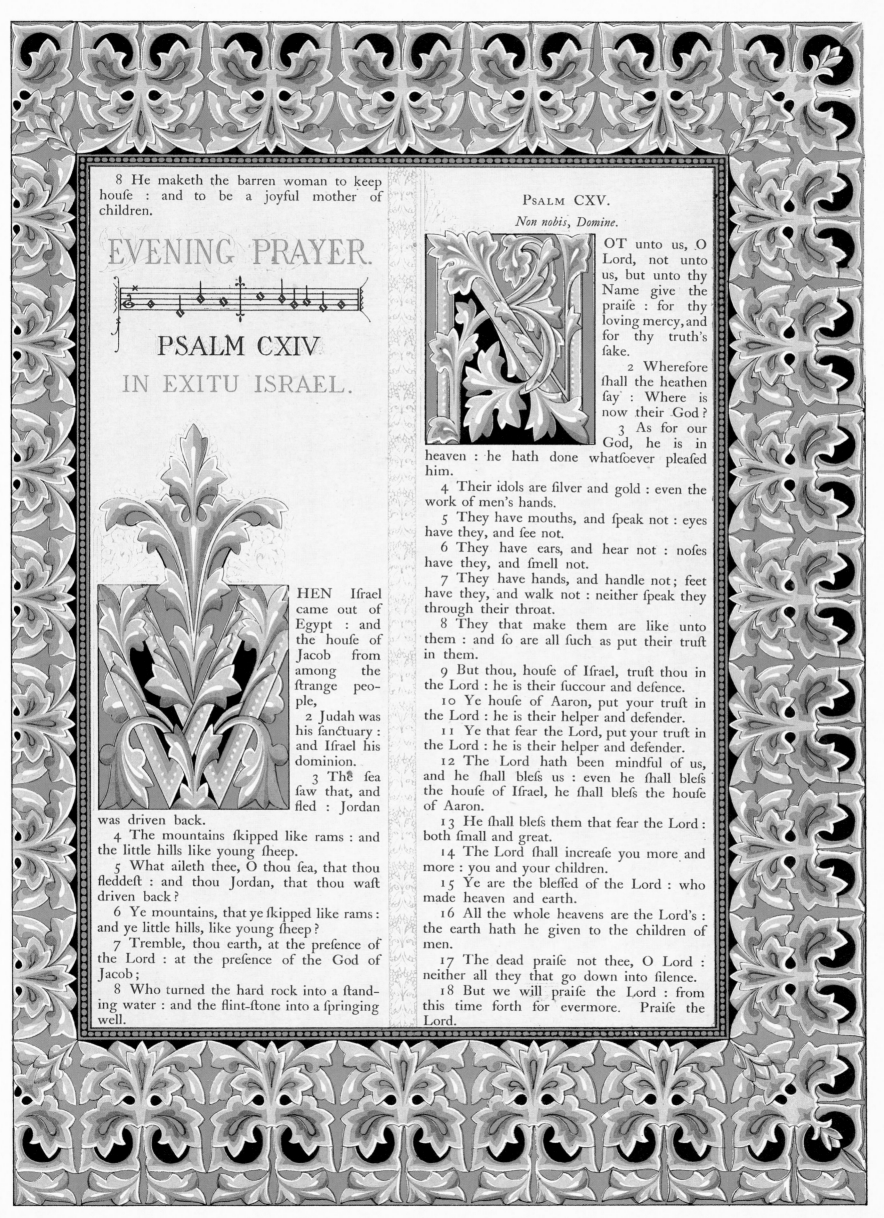

8 He maketh the barren woman to keep house : and to be a joyful mother of children.

EVENING PRAYER.

PSALM CXIV

IN EXITU ISRAEL.

HEN Israel came out of Egypt : and the house of Jacob from among the strange people,

2 Judah was his sanctuary : and Israel his dominion.

3 The sea saw that, and fled : Jordan was driven back.

4 The mountains skipped like rams : and the little hills like young sheep.

5 What aileth thee, O thou sea, that thou fleddest : and thou Jordan, that thou wast driven back?

6 Ye mountains, that ye skipped like rams : and ye little hills, like young sheep?

7 Tremble, thou earth, at the presence of the Lord : at the presence of the God of Jacob;

8 Who turned the hard rock into a standing water : and the flint-stone into a springing well.

PSALM CXV.
Non nobis, Domine.

OT unto us, O Lord, not unto us, but unto thy Name give the praise : for thy loving mercy, and for thy truth's sake.

2 Wherefore shall the heathen say : Where is now their God?

3 As for our God, he is in heaven : he hath done whatsoever pleased him.

4 Their idols are silver and gold : even the work of men's hands.

5 They have mouths, and speak not : eyes have they, and see not.

6 They have ears, and hear not : noses have they, and smell not.

7 They have hands, and handle not; feet have they, and walk not : neither speak they through their throat.

8 They that make them are like unto them : and so are all such as put their trust in them.

9 But thou, house of Israel, trust thou in the Lord : he is their succour and defence.

10 Ye house of Aaron, put your trust in the Lord : he is their helper and defender.

11 Ye that fear the Lord, put your trust in the Lord : he is their helper and defender.

12 The Lord hath been mindful of us, and he shall bless us : even he shall bless the house of Israel, he shall bless the house of Aaron.

13 He shall bless them that fear the Lord : both small and great.

14 The Lord shall increase you more and more : you and your children.

15 Ye are the blessed of the Lord : who made heaven and earth.

16 All the whole heavens are the Lord's : the earth hath he given to the children of men.

17 The dead praise not thee, O Lord : neither all they that go down into silence.

18 But we will praise the Lord : from this time forth for evermore. Praise the Lord.

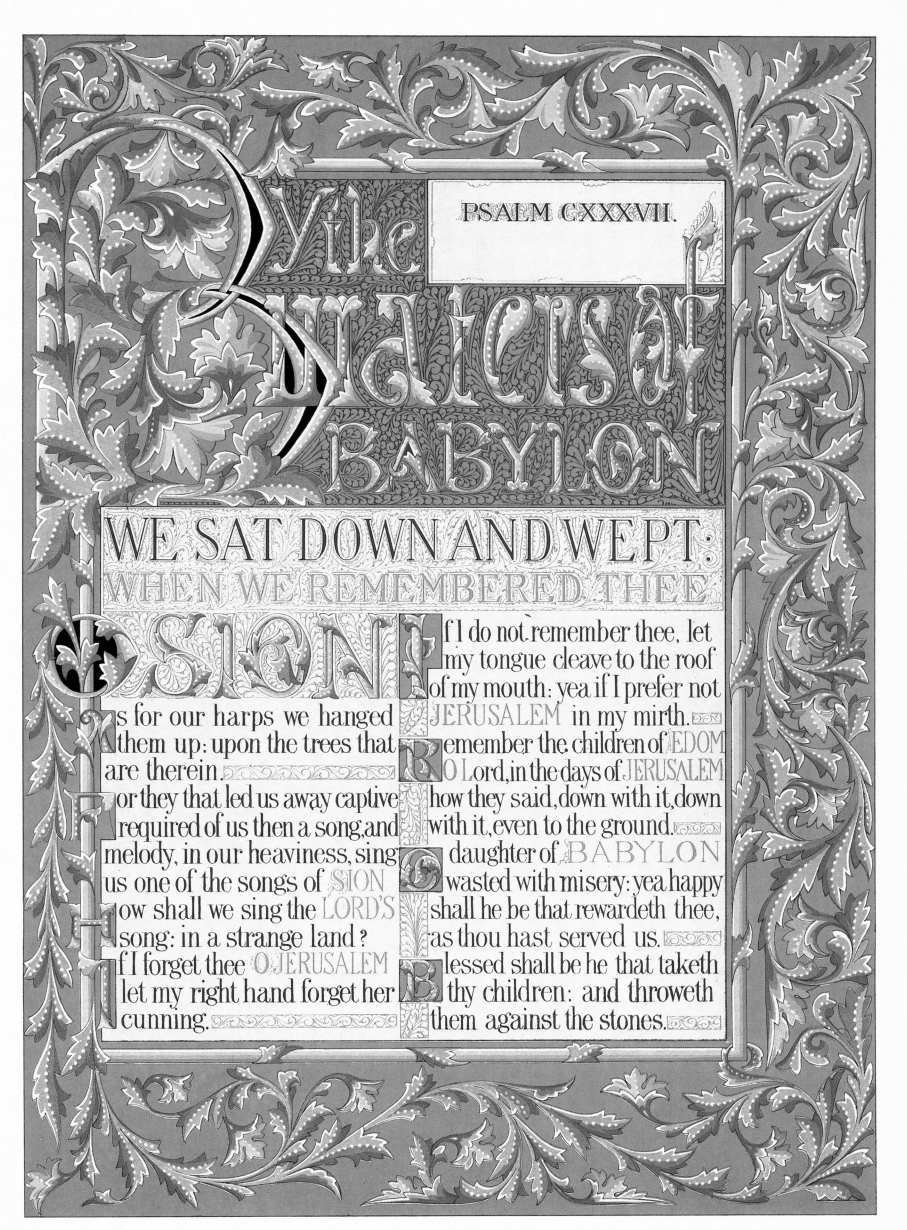

PSALM CXXXVII.

By the Waters of Babylon

WE SAT DOWN AND WEPT:
WHEN WE REMEMBERED THEE

O SION

As for our harps we hanged them up: upon the trees that are therein.

For they that led us away captive required of us then a song, and melody, in our heaviness, sing us one of the songs of Sion

How shall we sing the LORD'S song: in a strange land?

If I forget thee O JERUSALEM let my right hand forget her cunning.

If I do not remember thee, let my tongue cleave to the roof of my mouth: yea if I prefer not JERUSALEM in my mirth.

Remember the children of EDOM O Lord, in the days of JERUSALEM how they said, down with it, down with it, even to the ground.

O daughter of BABYLON wasted with misery: yea happy shall he be that rewardeth thee, as thou hast served us.

Blessed shall be he that taketh thy children: and throweth them against the stones.

Psalm CXXXVIII.

Confitebor tibi.

WILL give thanks unto thee, O Lord, with my whole heart : even before the gods will I sing praise unto thee.

2 I will worship toward thy holy temple, and praise thy Name, because of thy loving-kindness and truth : for thou haft magnified thy Name, and thy Word, above all things.

3 When I called upon thee, thou heardeft me : and enduedft my soul with much ftrength.

4 All the kings of the earth shall praise thee, O Lord : for they have heard the words of thy mouth.

5 Yea, they shall sing in the ways of the Lord : that great is the glory of the Lord.

6 For though the Lord be high, yet hath he respect unto the lowly : as for the proud, he beholdeth them afar off.

7 Though I walk in the midst of trouble, yet shalt thou refresh me : thou shalt stretch forth thy hand upon the furioufness of mine enemies, and thy right hand shall save me.

8 The Lord shall make good his loving-kindnefs toward me : yea, thy mercy, O Lord, endureth for ever ; despise not then the works of thine own hands.

MORNING PRAYER.

PSALM CXXXIX.

DOMINE PROBASTI.

LORD, thou haft searched me out, and known me : thou knoweft my down-fit-ting, and mine up-rising ; thou underftandeft my thoughts long before.

2 Thou art about my path, and about my bed : and fpieft out all my ways.

3 For lo, there is not a word in my tongue : but thou, O Lord, knoweft it altogether.

4 Thou haft fashioned me behind and before : and laid thine hand upon me.

5 Such knowledge is too wonderful and excellent for me : I cannot attain unto it.

6 Whither shall I go then from thy Spirit : or whither shall I go then from thy presence ?

7 If I climb up into heaven, thou art there : if I go down to hell, thou art there also.

8 If I take the wings of the morning : and remain in the uttermoft parts of the sea ;

9 Even there also shall thy hand lead me : and thy right hand shall hold me.

10 If I say, Peradventure the darknefs shall cover me : then shall my night be turned to day.

11 Yea, the darknefs is no darknefs with thee, but the night is as clear as the day : the darknefs and light to thee are both alike.

12 For my reins are thine : thou haft covered me in my mother's womb.

13 I will give thanks unto thee, for I am fearfully and wonderfully made : marvellous are thy works, and that my soul knoweth right well.

14 My bones are not hid from thee : though I be made secretly, and fashioned beneath in the earth.

15 Thine eyes did see my fubftance, yet being imperfect : and in thy book were all my members written ;

16 Which day by day were fashioned : when as yet there was none of them.

17 How dear are thy counsels unto me, O God : O how great is the sum of them !

18 If I tell them, they are more in number than the fand : when I wake up I am prefent with thee.

19 Wilt thou not slay the wicked, O God : depart from me, ye blood-thirfty men.

20 For they speak unrighteoufly againft thee : and thine enemies take thy Name in vain.

21 Do not I hate them, O Lord, that hate thee : and am not I grieved with those that rife up againft thee ?

22 Yea, I hate them right fore : even as though they were mine enemies.

23 Try me, O God, and seek the ground of my heart : prove me, and examine my thoughts.

24 Look well if there be any way of wickednefs in me : and lead me in the way everlafting.

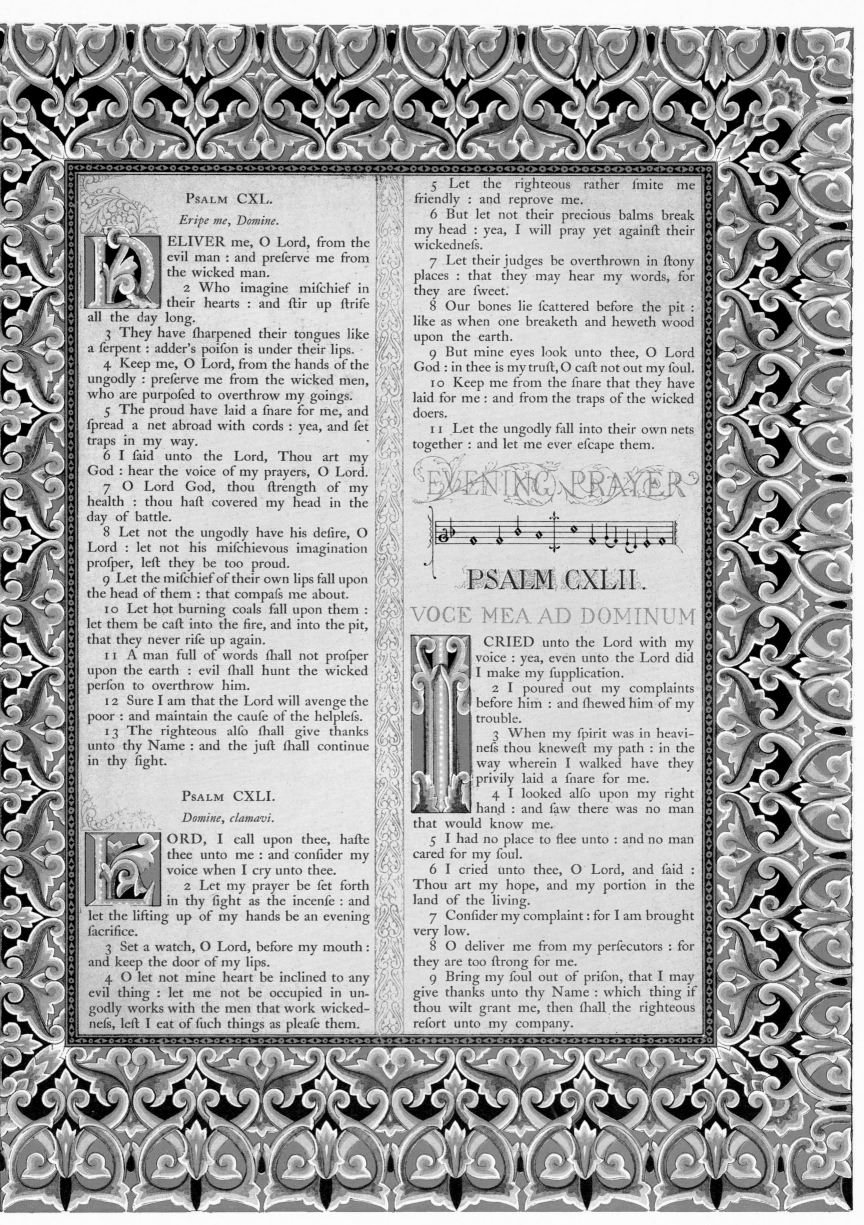

Psalm CXL.

Eripe me, Domine.

DELIVER me, O Lord, from the evil man : and preferve me from the wicked man.

2 Who imagine mifchief in their hearts : and ftir up ftrife all the day long.

3 They have fharpened their tongues like a ferpent : adder's poifon is under their lips.

4 Keep me, O Lord, from the hands of the ungodly : preferve me from the wicked men, who are purpofed to overthrow my goings.

5 The proud have laid a fnare for me, and fpread a net abroad with cords : yea, and fet traps in my way.

6 I faid unto the Lord, Thou art my God : hear the voice of my prayers, O Lord.

7 O Lord God, thou ftrength of my health : thou haft covered my head in the day of battle.

8 Let not the ungodly have his defire, O Lord : let not his mifchievous imagination profper, left they be too proud.

9 Let the mifchief of their own lips fall upon the head of them : that compafs me about.

10 Let hot burning coals fall upon them : let them be caft into the fire, and into the pit, that they never rife up again.

11 A man full of words fhall not profper upon the earth : evil fhall hunt the wicked perfon to overthrow him.

12 Sure I am that the Lord will avenge the poor : and maintain the caufe of the helplefs.

13 The righteous alfo fhall give thanks unto thy Name : and the juft fhall continue in thy fight.

Psalm CXLI.

Domine, clamavi.

LORD, I call upon thee, hafte thee unto me : and confider my voice when I cry unto thee.

2 Let my prayer be fet forth in thy fight as the incenfe : and let the lifting up of my hands be an evening facrifice.

3 Set a watch, O Lord, before my mouth : and keep the door of my lips.

4 O let not mine heart be inclined to any evil thing : let me not be occupied in ungodly works with the men that work wickednefs, left I eat of fuch things as pleafe them.

5 Let the righteous rather fmite me friendly : and reprove me.

6 But let not their precious balms break my head : yea, I will pray yet againft their wickednefs.

7 Let their judges be overthrown in ftony places : that they may hear my words, for they are fweet.

8 Our bones lie fcattered before the pit : like as when one breaketh and heweth wood upon the earth.

9 But mine eyes look unto thee, O Lord God : in thee is my truft, O caft not out my foul.

10 Keep me from the fnare that they have laid for me : and from the traps of the wicked doers.

11 Let the ungodly fall into their own nets together : and let me ever efcape them.

EVENING PRAYER

PSALM CXLII.

VOCE MEA AD DOMINUM

I CRIED unto the Lord with my voice : yea, even unto the Lord did I make my fupplication.

2 I poured out my complaints before him : and fhewed him of my trouble.

3 When my fpirit was in heavinefs thou kneweft my path : in the way wherein I walked have they privily laid a fnare for me.

4 I looked alfo upon my right hand : and faw there was no man that would know me.

5 I had no place to flee unto : and no man cared for my foul.

6 I cried unto thee, O Lord, and faid : Thou art my hope, and my portion in the land of the living.

7 Confider my complaint : for I am brought very low.

8 O deliver me from my perfecutors : for they are too ftrong for me.

9 Bring my foul out of prifon, that I may give thanks unto thy Name : which thing if thou wilt grant me, then fhall the righteous refort unto my company.

PSALM CXLIII.

DOMINE EXAUDI.

Hear my prayer, O Lord,

and consider my desire: hearken unto me for thy truth and righteousness' sake.

And enter not into judgement with thy servant for in thy sight shall no man living be justified.

3 For the enemy hath perfecuted my foul ; he hath fmitten my life down to the ground : he hath laid me in the darkneſs, as the men that have been long dead.

4 Therefore is my ſpirit vexed within me : and my heart within me is defolate.

5 Yet do I remember the time paſt ; I muſe upon all thy works : yea, I exerciſe myſelf in the works of thy hands.

6 I ſtretch forth my hands unto thee : my foul gaſpeth unto thee as a thirſty land.

7 Hear me, O Lord, and that ſoon, for my ſpirit waxeth faint : hide not thy face from me, leſt I be like unto them that go down into the pit.

8 O let me hear thy loving-kindneſs betimes in the morning, for in thee is my truſt : ſhew thou me the way that I ſhould walk in, for I lift up my foul unto thee.

9 Deliver me, O Lord, from mine enemies : for I flee unto thee to hide me.

10 Teach me to do the thing that pleaſeth thee, for thou art my God : let thy loving Spirit lead me forth into the land of righteouſneſs.

11 Quicken me, O Lord, for thy Name's fake : and for thy righteouſneſs' fake bring my foul out of trouble.

12 And of thy goodneſs ſlay mine enemies : and deſtroy all them that vex my foul ; for I am thy ſervant.

MORNING PRAYER.

PSALM CXLIV.

BENEDICTUS DOMINUS.

LESSED be the Lord my ſtrength : who teacheth my hands to war, and my fingers to fight ;

2 My hope and my fortreſs, my caſtle and deliverer, my defender in whom I truſt : who ſubdueth my people that is under me.

3 Lord, what is man, that thou haſt ſuch reſpect unto him : or the ſon of man, that thou ſo regardeſt him ?

4 Man is like a thing of nought : his time paſſeth away like a ſhadow.

5 Bow thy heavens, O Lord, and come down : touch the mountains, and they ſhall ſmoke.

6 Caſt forth thy lightning, and tear them : ſhoot out thine arrows, and conſume them.

7 Send down thine hand from above : deliver me, and take me out of the great waters, from the hand of ſtrange children ;

8 Whoſe mouth talketh of vanity : and their right hand is a right hand of wickedneſs.

9 I will ſing a new ſong unto thee, O God : and ſing praiſes unto thee upon a ten-ſtringed lute.

10 Thou haſt given victory unto kings : and haſt delivered David thy ſervant from the peril of the ſword.

11 Save me, and deliver me from the hand of ſtrange children : whoſe mouth talketh of vanity, and their right hand is a right hand of iniquity.

12 That our ſons may grow up as the young plants : and that our daughters may be as the poliſhed corners of the temple.

13 That our garners may be full and plenteous with all manner of ſtore : that our ſheep may bring forth thouſands and ten thouſands in our ſtreets.

14 That our oxen may be ſtrong to labour, that there be no decay : no leading into captivity, and no complaining in our ſtreets.

15 Happy are the people that are in ſuch a caſe : yea, bleſſed are the people who have the Lord for their God.

Psalm CXLV.

Exaltabo te, Deus.

WILL magnify thee, O God, my King : and I will praiſe thy Name for ever and ever.

2 Every day will I give thanks unto thee : and praiſe thy Name for ever and ever.

3 Great is the Lord, and marvellous, worthy to be praiſed : there is no end of his greatneſs.

4 One generation ſhall praiſe thy works unto another : and declare thy power.

5 As for me, I will be talking of thy worſhip : thy glory, thy praiſe, and wondrous works ;

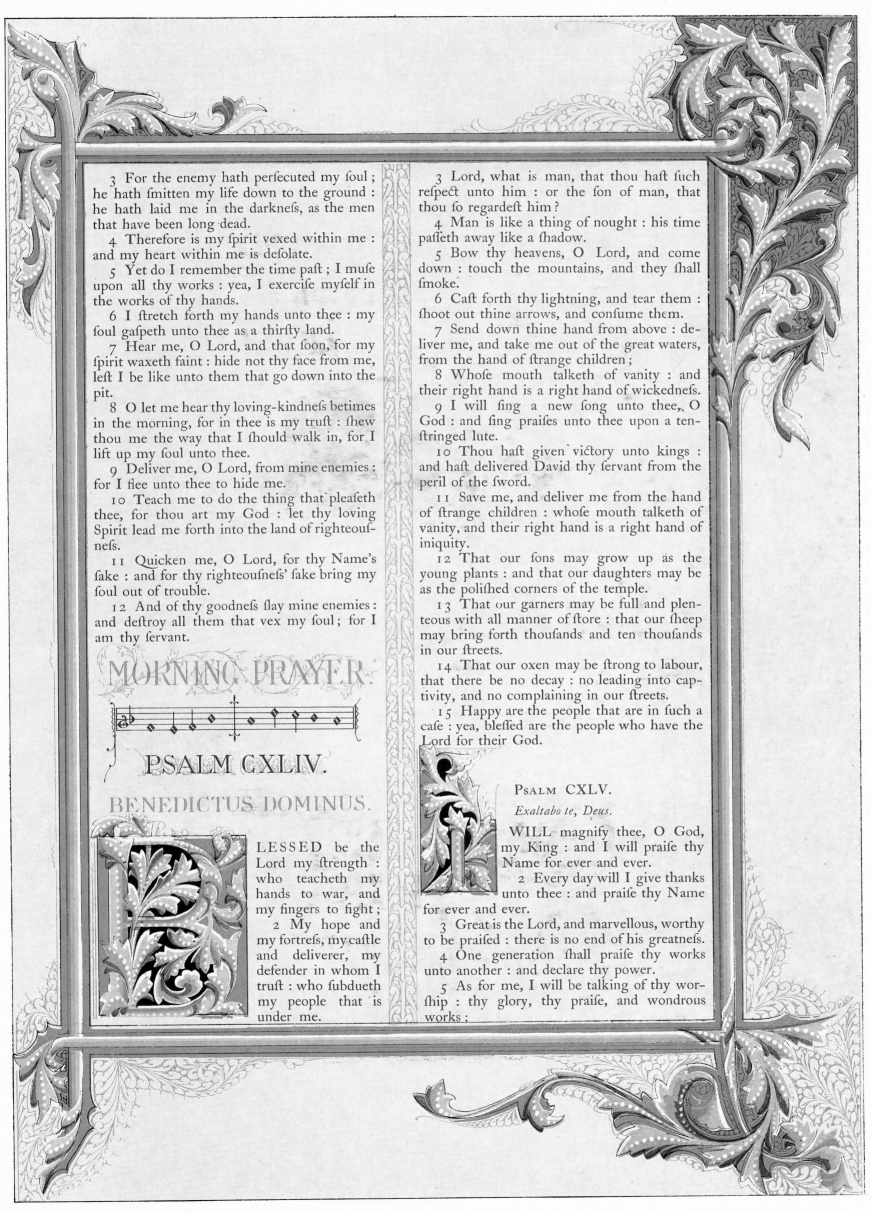

6 So that men shall speak of the might of thy marvellous acts : and I will also tell of thy greatness.

7 The memorial of thine abundant kindness shall be shewed : and men shall sing of thy righteousness.

8 The Lord is gracious, and merciful : long-suffering, and of great goodness.

9 The Lord is loving unto every man : and his mercy is over all his works.

10 All thy works praise thee, O Lord : and thy saints give thanks unto thee.

11 They shew the glory of thy kingdom : and talk of thy power.

12 That thy power, thy glory, and mightiness of thy kingdom : might be known unto men.

13 Thy kingdom is an everlasting kingdom : and thy dominion endureth throughout all ages.

14 The Lord upholdeth all such as fall : and lifteth up all those that are down.

15 The eyes of all wait upon thee, O Lord : and thou givest them their meat in due season.

16 Thou openest thine hand : and fillest all things living with plenteousness.

17 The Lord is righteous in all his ways : and holy in all his works.

18 The Lord is nigh unto all them that call upon him : yea, all such as call upon him faithfully.

19 He will fulfil the desire of them that fear him : he also will hear their cry, and will help them.

20 The Lord preserveth all them that love him : but scattereth abroad all the ungodly.

21 My mouth shall speak the praise of the Lord : and let all flesh give thanks unto his holy Name for ever and ever.

Psalm CXLVI.

Lauda, anima mea.

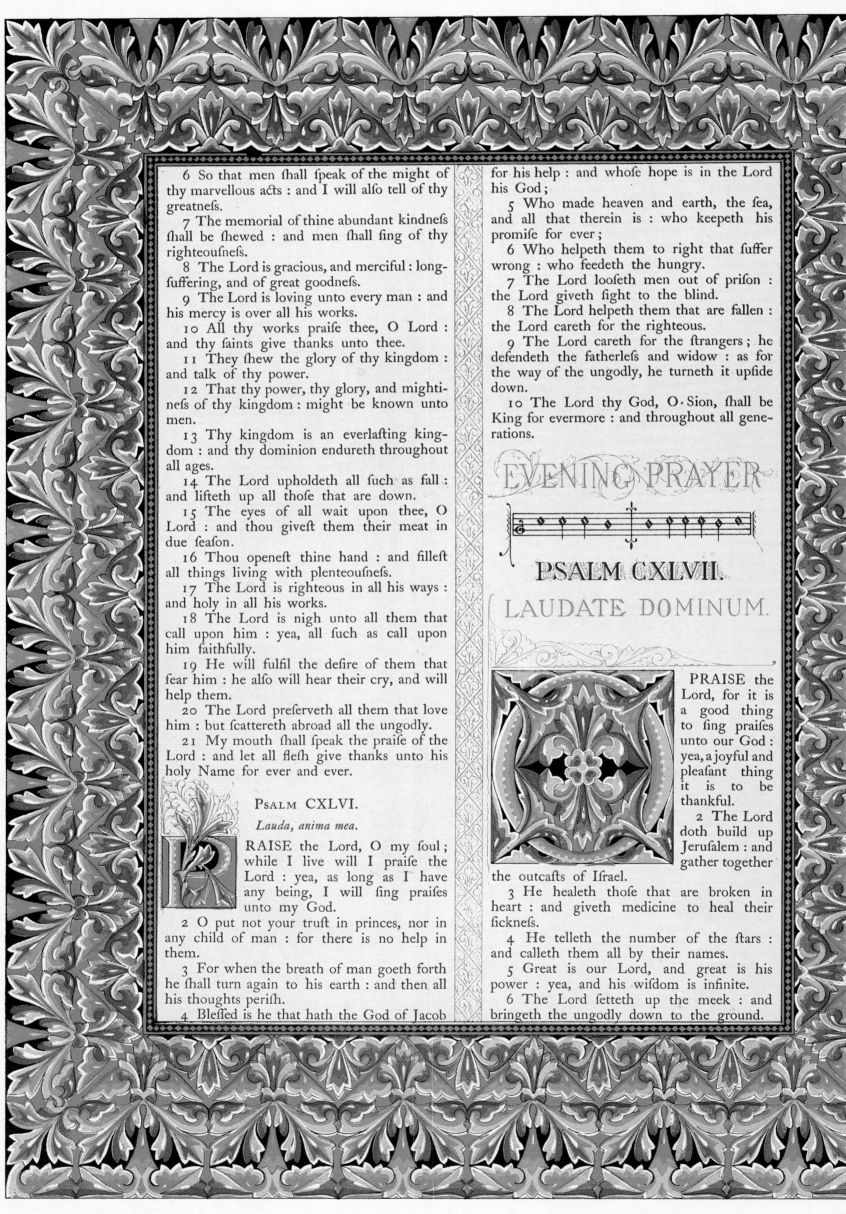

PRAISE the Lord, O my soul; while I live will I praise the Lord : yea, as long as I have any being, I will sing praises unto my God.

2 O put not your trust in princes, nor in any child of man : for there is no help in them.

3 For when the breath of man goeth forth he shall turn again to his earth : and then all his thoughts perish.

4 Blessed is he that hath the God of Jacob for his help : and whose hope is in the Lord his God;

5 Who made heaven and earth, the sea, and all that therein is : who keepeth his promise for ever;

6 Who helpeth them to right that suffer wrong : who feedeth the hungry.

7 The Lord looseth men out of prison : the Lord giveth sight to the blind.

8 The Lord helpeth them that are fallen : the Lord careth for the righteous.

9 The Lord careth for the strangers ; he defendeth the fatherless and widow : as for the way of the ungodly, he turneth it upside down.

10 The Lord thy God, O Sion, shall be King for evermore : and throughout all generations.

EVENING PRAYER

PSALM CXLVII.

LAUDATE DOMINUM.

PRAISE the Lord, for it is a good thing to sing praises unto our God : yea, a joyful and pleasant thing it is to be thankful.

2 The Lord doth build up Jerusalem : and gather together the outcasts of Israel.

3 He healeth those that are broken in heart : and giveth medicine to heal their sickness.

4 He telleth the number of the stars : and calleth them all by their names.

5 Great is our Lord, and great is his power : yea, and his wisdom is infinite.

6 The Lord setteth up the meek : and bringeth the ungodly down to the ground.

7 O sing unto the Lord with thanksgiving : sing praises upon the harp unto our God ;

8 Who covereth the heaven with clouds, and prepareth rain for the earth : and maketh the grass to grow upon the mountains, and herb for the use of men ;

9 Who giveth fodder unto the cattle : and feedeth the young ravens that call upon him.

10 He hath no pleasure in the strength of an horse : neither delighteth he in any man's legs.

11 But the Lord's delight is in them that fear him : and put their trust in his mercy.

12 Praise the Lord, O Jerusalem : praise thy God, O Sion.

13 For he hath made fast the bars of thy gates : and hath blessed thy children within thee.

14 He maketh peace in thy borders : and filleth thee with the flour of wheat.

15 He sendeth forth his commandment upon earth : and his word runneth very swiftly.

16 He giveth snow like wool : and scattereth the hoar-frost like ashes.

17 He casteth forth his ice like morsels : who is able to abide his frost ?

18 He sendeth out his word, and melteth them : he bloweth with his wind, and the waters flow.

19 He sheweth his word unto Jacob : his statutes and ordinances unto Israel.

20 He hath not dealt so with any nation : neither have the heathen knowledge of his laws.

Psalm CXLVIII.

Laudate Dominum.

PRAISE the Lord of heaven : praise him in the height.

2 Praise him, all ye angels of his : praise him, all his host.

3 Praise him, sun and moon : praise him, all ye stars and light.

4 Praise him, all ye heavens : and ye waters that are above the heavens.

5 Let them praise the Name of the Lord : for he spake the word, and they were made ; he commanded, and they were created.

6 He hath made them fast for ever and ever : he hath given them a law which shall not be broken.

7 Praise the Lord upon earth : ye dragons, and all deeps ;

8 Fire and hail, snow and vapours : wind and storm, fulfilling his word ;

9 Mountains and all hills : fruitful trees and all cedars ;

10 Beasts and all cattle : worms and feathered fowls ;

11 Kings of the earth and all people : princes and all judges of the world ;

12 Young men and maidens, old men and children, praise the Name of the Lord : for his Name only is excellent, and his praise above heaven and earth.

13 He shall exalt the horn of his people ; all his saints shall praise him : even the children of Israel, even the people that serveth him.

Psalm CXLIX.

Cantate Domino.

SING unto the Lord a new song : let the congregation of saints praise him.

2 Let Israel rejoice in him that made him : and let the children of Sion be joyful in their King.

3 Let them praise his Name in the dance : let them sing praises unto him with tabret and harp.

4 For the Lord hath pleasure in his people : and helpeth the meek-hearted.

5 Let the saints be joyful with glory : let them rejoice in their beds.

6 Let the praises of God be in their mouth : and a two-edged sword in their hands ;

7 To be avenged of the heathen : and to rebuke the people ;

8 To bind their kings in chains : and their nobles with links of iron.

9 That they may be avenged of them, as it is written : Such honour have all his saints.

Psalm CL.

Laudate Dominum.

PRAISE God in his holiness : praise him in the firmament of his power.

2 Praise him in his noble acts : praise him according to his excellent greatness.

3 Praise him in the sound of the trumpet : praise him upon the lute and harp.

4 Praise him in the cymbals and dances : praise him upon the strings and pipe.

5 Praise him upon the well-tuned cymbals : praise him upon the loud cymbals.

6 Let every thing that hath breath : praise the Lord.

PAGE C.